TEACHING PSYCHOLOGY 14–19

Teaching Psychology 14–19 – first published as *Teaching Post-16 Psychology* – is a core text for all training psychology teachers, as well as experienced teachers engaged in further study and professional development. Taking a reflective approach, Matt Jarvis explores key issues and debates against a backdrop of research and theory, and provides guidance on practical ideas intended to make life in the psychology classroom easier.

With an emphasis on the application of psychology to teaching psychology, it clearly and comprehensively covers the knowledge essential to develop as a successful teacher. Key issues considered include:

- the appeal of psychology and what the subject can offer students
- the psychology curriculum and advice on how to choose a syllabus
- principles of effective teaching and learning
- teaching psychological thinking
- differentiated psychology teaching
- choosing and developing resources
- using technology effectively.

With a new chapter exploring the role of practical work in the post-coursework era, this second edition considers psychology teaching across the 14–19 age range and has been updated in light of the latest research, policy and practice in the field.

Teaching Psychology 14–19 is an essential text for all those engaged in enhancing their understanding of teaching psychology in the secondary school.

Matt Jarvis leads the PGCE Psychology at Keele University, UK.

TEACHING PSYCHOLOGY 14–19

Issues and techniques

Matt Jarvis

LONDON AND NEW YORK

First published 2006
by Nelson Thornes Ltd
Delta Place, 27 Bath Road, Cheltenham, GL53 7TH

This edition published 2011
by Routledge
2 Park Square, Milton Park, Abingdon, Oxon OX14 4RN

Simultaneously published in the USA and Canada
by Routledge
711 Third Avenue, New York, NY 10017

*Routledge is an imprint of the Taylor & Francis Group, an informa
business*

British Library Cataloguing in Publication Data
A catalogue record for this book is available from the British Library

Library of Congress Cataloging-in-Publication Data
Jarvis, Matt, 1966-
Teaching psychology 14-19 : issues & techniques / Matt Jarvis.
    p. cm.
    Rev. ed. of: Teaching post-16 psychology. 2006.
    1. Psychology--Study and teaching (Higher)--Great Britain.
    2. Psychology--Study and teaching (Higher) I. Jarvis, Matt, 1966-
    Teaching post-16 psychology. II. Title. III. Title: Teaching psychology
    fourteen-nineteen.
    BF77.J37 2011   150.71--dc22
    2010053803

ISBN: 978-0-415-67025-8 (hbk)
ISBN: 978-0-415-67026-5 (pbk)
ISBN: 978-0-203-81017-0 (ebk)

Typeset in Times New Roman and Helvetica Neue
by Bookcraft Ltd

MIX
Paper from
responsible sources
FSC   FSC® C004839
www.fsc.org

Printed and bound in Great Britain by
TJ International Ltd, Padstow, Cornwall

CONTENTS

FIGURES

BOXES

TABLES

PREFACE TO THE NEW EDITION

Welcome! I hope that both new and experienced teachers of psychology will enjoy and draw something useful from this book. My aim in writing it was to provide some practical ideas to make life in the psychology classroom easier and more interesting, but also to set those ideas in a context of psychological theory and research – in other words to apply psychology to teaching psychology.

The political context in which we teach has changed considerably since the first edition of this book – then titled *Teaching Post-16 Psychology* – was published in 2006. The relentless focus on attainment in education and the resulting redefinitions of ideas such as 'effectiveness' and 'good practice' *may* have contributed to social mobility – the jury is still out on that one – but have certainly had unintended negative consequences for teachers and students. In this edition, slightly reluctantly, I have felt obliged to set advice in this political context as well as the psychological. A theme running throughout the book concerns the tension between holistic and strategic teaching – the former considering the student experience and holistic development and the latter being oriented purely towards attainment.

Inevitably some teachers reading this will be interested in sinking their teeth into more esoteric issues of politics and psychological theory, while many others will simply be looking for practical classroom ideas. That's very healthy. I would defend the use of theory to strict pragmatists on the basis that setting techniques in theoretical context helps us understand *why* they work and so how to adapt them and recreate their effective features in different contexts. If you are undertaking Master's-level study this way of thinking will be essential.

Chapter 1 is rather philosophical, as I consider issues like the appeal of psychology, what psychology can provide students with and what makes a good teacher. However if you're primarily interested in practical stuff don't be put off – the book becomes more applied as it goes on. In Chapter 2 I look at the psychology curriculum and provide some advice on how to choose a syllabus, defend the rigour of psychology and benchmark yourself properly. In Chapter 3 I look at what makes for effective teaching, using research and examples from the psychology teaching literature. Chapter 4 is new for this edition, focusing on the issues surrounding practical work in the post-coursework era. Chapter 5 is concerned with strategies to help students to think 'psychologically'. In Chapter 6 I consider resourcing issues, including how to choose a textbook, what other sources of published literature to make use of and some hints for developing your own handouts and worksheets. Chapter 7 deals with using technology to enhance the psychology classroom, and I present some ideas on ways to incorporate – standard and not so standard – ICT into psychology lessons. Finally, in Chapter 8, I look at diversity in the needs of psychology students and make some suggestions for differentiation.

One thing I want to make very clear at the outset is the spirit in which the ideas presented here are offered. They are there to stimulate and challenge, and to be drawn upon as required. There is no implication that we should all constantly be using all the techniques discussed here, just that they may prove useful. If, for example, you want to further develop your use of learning technology, you may find something helpful in Chapter 7. I have also felt free to offer views on controversial issues in the belief that the distinction between information and opinion is clear, and that readers will make up their own minds where they stand on controversies. In these days of eroded teacher autonomy and sometimes oppressive quality assurance it is important that teachers are armed with the sort of information and argument that allows us to take a lead in developing professional practice. I hope this helps.

CHAPTER 1

THE PHILOSOPHY BIT: WHO, WHAT AND WHY?

By the end of this chapter you should be able to:

- Explain some of the reasons why students opt to study psychology, with particular reference to perceived rigour, intrinsic interest and potential therapeutic value.
- Assess the potential benefits for students of studying psychology with particular regard to transferable skills and preparation to study psychology at degree level.
- Appreciate the tension between catering for the short- and long-term needs of psychology students.
- Apply research findings into reasons for and benefits of studying psychology to enhancing classroom practice.
- Discuss the attributes of an effective psychology teacher.
- Consider the concept of reflective practice as a model for understanding the developing psychology teacher.
- Discuss the role of evidence-based practice in psychology teaching.
- Be aware of the breadth of ways in which psychology can be applied to teaching psychology.

This book contains a blend of theory, research and practical advice. If you are reading purely for the top tips you may prefer to skip this chapter. This is a chance to step back from the practicalities of the classroom to think a bit more broadly about the philosophy of psychology teaching – what we are here for. This isn't meant to be an indulgence, but is rather based on the belief that practical ideas can be born, not necessarily from theory or research, but certainly from having a broader understanding of what we do. What are psychology teachers here for? What do students hope to get from studying psychology? What makes any teacher effective? It is extremely difficult for teachers to find space in the teaching day to escape the minutiae of planning, teaching, marking and admin and focus on these 'big picture' issues. It is, however, possible to at least consider these questions with reference to the psychology teaching literature.

A useful starting point is to consider why students choose to study psychology and what the potential benefits are of studying the subject. There is a body of research addressing both these issues and some clear implications for shaping classroom practice. In order to help achieve some of the ambitious goals suggested by this research I explore what makes an effective psychology teacher – while at the same time thinking critically about the notion of effectiveness. In the remainder of this chapter I consider two rather different ways of thinking about the practice of psychology teaching; reflective practice and evidence-based practice. Reflective practice has become a byword for quality in education, while evidence-based practice has enjoyed similar status in psychology for some time, and is becoming increasingly important in education. Psychology teachers, with a foot in both the psychology and education camps, are in an excellent position of being able to appreciate and draw on ideas from both reflective and evidence-based practice.

WHY DO PEOPLE STUDY PSYCHOLOGY?

The rapid growth in the popularity of psychology, particularly at post-16 and under-graduate levels, has not gone unnoticed in either psychology or education circles. We are no longer 'slipping under the radar' (Jarvis, 2007), and this presents opportunities in the form of funding – but also challenges to justify our popularity. Three major hypotheses have emerged from discussions. The rigour hypothesis is the idea that psychology is, or is at least perceived by students as being, an 'easier' A-level, and so students choose it in the belief that they will gain a high grade with relatively little effort. The intrinsic interest or 'sexy subject' hypothesis posits that psychology is seen as a particularly interesting subject, and that this interest is students' primary motiva-tion. The therapy hypothesis emphasises the appeal of psychology to those seeking personal insight into their own existential, psychosocial or mental health issues.

Rigour hypothesis

More conservative elements in the education establishment believe that students see psychology as an easy A-level, and that this is important in accounting for its current popularity. We can call this the rigour hypothesis. Those who argue this often cite a now-dated study by Fitz-Gibbon and Vincent (1994) showing that, at that time, students tended to score on average half a grade higher in psychology than in the most difficult subjects.

There is, however, wide agreement now that the rigour hypothesis is flawed; apart from anything else the statistical evidence taken from more recent A-level cohorts is strongly supportive of psychology as a rigorous A-level (see Morris, 2003; Jarvis, 2004; and Chapter 2 for detailed discussions). Moreover, student surveys have found no evidence to suggest that they perceive psychology as an easy subject. On the contrary, Hirschler and Banyard (2003) report that 43% of post-16 students surveyed described psychology as more difficult than their other subjects, with 30% describing it as equally difficult and only 27% finding it easier.

Sexy subject hypothesis

In fact, studies have clearly shown that the overwhelming factor influencing students' choice of psychology is its fit with our current cultural ideas of what is inherently interesting. In other words it is seen as 'sexy'. In one survey, Hirschler and Banyard (2003) surveyed 454 post-16 level-3 psychology students – all but 17 were studying A-level. Three factors emerged as particularly important in the decision to study psychology: interest; preparation for a career in psychology; and the novelty value attached to a subject not previously studied. Table 1.1 shows the percentages.

In this study, interest value emerged as the most popular response and no other factors were mentioned by more than 1% of respondents. Encouragingly, pre-study perceptions of psychology as an interesting subject were borne out by students' experiences. The majority rated it as more interesting than their other subjects. A breakdown of responses is shown in Table 1.2.

Walker (2004) has extended this line of research by breaking down further the idea of interest. Based on a content analysis of responses to the open question 'why do you want to study AS psychology?', Walker has identified five distinct aspects of interest:

■   Interest in people
■   Interest in subject matter

■ **Table 1.1** Reasons for choosing psychology (Hirschler and Banyard, 2003)

Rank	Primary reason	%
1	Sounded interesting	64
2	Want a career in psychology	19
3	Something different to study	11

■ **Table 1.2** Perceptions of interest value of psychology (Hirschler and Banyard, 2003)

Response	%
Much more interesting	44
Slightly more interesting	36
About the same	15
Slightly less interesting	3
Much less interesting	2

- ■ Novelty interest
- ■ Career interest
- ■ Personal issues

When students and teachers were asked to rank these in order of importance there was a surprising level of agreement, interest in people and subject interest emerging as the most important factors. Figure 1.1 shows student and teacher mean rankings.

Therapy hypothesis

It has long been believed by many post-16 psychology teachers that they have attracted a disproportionate number of students with mental health problems, and that these students have chosen to study psychology in an attempt – conscious or unconscious – to seek insight into their conditions. This has sometimes been called the therapy hypothesis. There is no doubt that many students with mental health problems do derive benefit from studying psychology, nor that for some this is an important factor in their subject choice. However, there is little direct evidence that psychology attracts particularly large numbers of students with mental health problems. Teachers' folk beliefs concerning this may be largely an artefact of greater disclosure rates in the context of psychology where the lesson content cues such disclosure. Surveys of students' subject choice-motives such as those of Hirschler and Banyard (2003) and Walker (2010) have not revealed significant numbers of

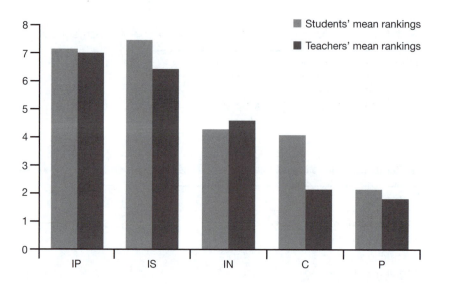

■ **Figure 1.1** Student and teacher rankings of interest factors (from Walker, 2010)

students suggesting that their subject choice was motivated by therapy-seeking. Indeed, Walker went on to directly investigate the therapy hypothesis by means of interviewing students, and in no case did his participants report a therapeutic motive.

WHAT ARE THE POTENTIAL BENEFITS OF STUDYING POST-16 PSYCHOLOGY?

This question has been approached from a number of angles in the psychology teaching literature. There is clear evidence that what students seek primarily from studying psychology is interest, and that in this sense they are widely satisfied. However, there may be additional long-term benefits from studying psychology, both in terms of preparation for studying psychology in higher education (HE) and acquiring generic study and employment skills.

Preparation for HE psychology

Prior to the 1990s there was a consensus that studying psychology at school or college was unhelpful in terms of preparation for study at undergraduate level, and that those hoping to study for a psychology degree should at all costs avoid psychology A-level. With the explosion of numbers studying psychology – in particular A-level – in the 1990s this view rapidly became untenable.

There is nonetheless still some ambivalence around among HE teachers towards psychology A-level. One professor of psychology has spoken of the difficulty of teaching students 'acculturated into psychology A-level' (anon, personal communication). Conway (2007) blamed attitudes in HE on the mismatch between the psychology curriculum at pre-degree and undergraduate level and called for a 'standard scientific and representative curriculum' at A-level. However, as Green (2005) pointed out, there has always been a lack of clarity over the purpose of A-level; is it meant to prepare students for HE or for employment? Unless we take the view that psychology at school and college exists solely or primarily to prepare students for study of psychology at undergraduate level, it is unreasonable to subjugate the curriculum to the needs of an HE lobby, even assuming a consensus emerged about what such a curriculum should look like – which it hasn't.

HE ambivalence aside, common sense suggests that students who have already studied psychology enter a degree with a better idea of what to expect and so have some advantage. In response to this situation, the British Psychological Society (BPS) undertook two studies, one involving HE teachers and the other students. Banister (2003) surveyed the Heads of Psychology at 25 UK universities about their perceptions of and policies towards prior psychology qualifications. In the majority of departments (15) psychology qualifications were not a factor in the admissions process, although a minority (5) did specify that some psychology background was helpful for mature students. In a clear majority of departments (18), prior qualifications in psychology were neither encouraged nor discouraged. Perhaps the most interesting findings concerned the advantages or otherwise for psychology students of having a prior qualification. Although in raw figures students with psychology A-level did slightly worse on research methods and statistics courses than others, once GCSE and A-level score were controlled for they did slightly better – students with psychology typically had worse qualifications overall. There is thus probably some advantage in having a psychology qualification for HE study. However, there was some concern expressed that students with a post-16 psychology qualification were at risk of coasting in their first year of undergraduate study and so acquiring bad study habits.

In the second BPS study, Linnell (2003) surveyed second-year undergraduate psychology students about their perceptions of pre-degree experience. Although attitudes were more positive among those who had previously studied psychology, overall students felt that post-16 psychology was helpful to studying undergraduate psychology. Percentages are shown below in Table 1.3.

Students in the Linnell study were acutely aware of the differences between post-16 and university teaching. Some commented that, in light of their university experience, they now considered their earlier teaching poor. On the other hand, others bemoaned the lack of opportunity for class discussion and the narrow focus on research methods and replicating classic studies required in undergraduate study.

Development of generic skills

The 1997 Dearing Report[1] highlighted a need for the curriculum at post-16 and undergraduate levels to address more effectively the development of generic skills in students as well as their subject knowledge. The six key skills that came out of the Dearing Report are still embedded throughout the curriculum, including in psychology specifications:

- Communication
- Application of number
- IT
- Working with others

■ **Table 1.3** Psychology undergraduates' beliefs about post-16 psychology (Linnell, 2003)

Item	% yes (no psychology qualification)	% yes (psychology qualification)
Helped with study skills	61	92
Helped with understanding	78	94
Improved grades	67	78
Improved motivation	33	66
More enjoyable	48	76

■ Improving own learning and performance
■ Problem solving.

Following the influential work of Carol McGuinness (1999), there is now an additional emphasis on developing a number of thinking skills throughout the curriculum:

■ Information-processing skills, including classifying, sequencing and comparing
■ Reasoning skills, including making inferences and judgements
■ Enquiry skills, including defining problems and planning research
■ Creative thinking skills, including generating hypotheses and ways to test them
■ Evaluation skills, including forming judgements of their own and others' work.

These broadly reflect the skills that psychology teachers expect to help develop during their teaching. In fact, psychology is arguably best placed of any discipline to address the full range of these skills. Key skills and thinking skills are addressed throughout this book, through whole chapters on developing psychological thinking and use of ICT, but also through problem-based learning, practical work and co-operative learning.

It is likely, of course, that the situation with regard to transferable skills changes with each incarnation of the curriculum. Curriculum 2000 drastically reduced the emphasis on essay-based assessment, with the result that teachers spent far less time developing essay-writing skills. In Curriculum 2008, coursework was removed from psychology, and with it the opportunity to develop creative, enquiry and communication skills. At the time of writing, the government has called for a return to more essay-based assessment, but we are awaiting clarification of how this will manifest.

LESSONS FROM THE RESEARCH: WHAT SHOULD PSYCHOLOGY TEACHING GIVE STUDENTS?

A balance between proximal and distal aims of teaching

Quality assurance mechanisms tend to encourage teachers to think exclusively in terms of outcome measures such as achievement by grade percentages. This is particularly true now that the Coalition Government has made clear its emphasis on outcome data in the form of raw attainment (Gove, 2010). Clearly grades are important, not least in encouraging social mobility, and we would not be doing well by our students if we abandoned exam preparation altogether to pursue more esoteric ideals in the classroom.

This much is obvious. There are, however, two factors that might militate against adopting a purely strategic grade-driven model of psychology teaching with an exclusive focus on drilling students for formal assessments. First, while psychology teaching has a proximal purpose in gaining the student a post-16 quali-fication, we are also responsible in some measure for what happens to students in the future. To put it bluntly, if we genuinely care in June we should still care in September; undergraduates and new entrants to employment are not an out-group, simply our 6th formers after the summer holiday. Teaching also has long-term or distal purposes in the form of developing transferable skills and fostering the enthusiasm to sustain students at the next level. We can gain students good exam grades by rushing them through a formularised process, but this is likely to be at the cost of both enthusiasm and skills.

The second caution against purely strategic teaching concerns motivation. Extrinsic motivation undermines intrinsic motivation, and in the same way as athletes' performance often worsens when they turn professional, we risk a loss of performance when we over-emphasise attainment to our students. To get the most from students it is essential that they receive the things psychology promises at the outset.

Make psychology interesting and relevant

This is in some ways so obvious that it might sound crass. Most students take up psychology for the sake of interest and the majority do find it interesting. However, this does not mean that every topic is always taught in such a way as to maximise its interest value, nor that every option is equally interesting to students. Experience tells us that in general it is theory and research with a clear real-world implication or application that arouses student interest. Every time a theory is taught, given a finite limit on the total volume of information students should take away, there is a trade-off to manage between the level of theoretical detail and the time left for real-world implications/applications. To maximise the interest value that can be obtained from a topic, try to avoid thinking 'how much theoretical detail should I teach for students to have the sort of understanding I'd like?' and think instead 'how little theoretical detail can I get away with teaching within the constraints of the nature of the assessment if students are to have a satisfactory understanding?' The latter approach may help free up time to focus on making the topic interesting, which in turn will probably lead to its being deeper processed and better remem-bered. The theme of how to maximise the interest value of psychology is a recur-ring one in this book. Examples of strategies include applying theory and research to understanding real-life scenarios (see p48), making reference to popular culture, for example in psychoanalytic interpretation or content analysis of television programmes (p101).

Consider the particular needs of future psychology undergraduates

In the Linnell (2003) survey study a number of undergraduate students reported that they found the transition from post-16 to undergraduate level difficult and would have welcomed more support. It was also clear that opinion varied as to how useful post-16 psychology was as a preparation for a psychology degree. Banister (2003) reported that studying post-16 psychology was less associated with good essay skills than was studying other subjects. The current A-level curriculum eschews report-writing and has cut essay-writing to a minimum. Although these changes have probably had benefits in terms of widening participation and increasing the reliability and validity of assessment, in terms of preparation for HE they have been disastrous.

It is clear that, although opportunities exist to help prepare psychology students for HE, generic teaching does not necessarily constitute effective preparation. Of course, responsibility for the post-16–degree transition does not lie exclusively with psychology teachers, and it can be difficult to reconcile the proximal aim of preparing for A-level exams with the more distal aim of preparing a minority of students for a psychology degree. Nonetheless, there are some things that post-16 teachers can do to lessen the culture shock of moving to higher education. Some examples are shown in Box 1.1.

If you are concerned about preparing students for a psychology degree but these activities seem too radical a departure from your usual teaching, consider writing a short tailored course for future psychology undergraduates. The Open College Network accredits short courses of at least 30 notional hours, and schools and colleges will have – although may not advertise – a budget dedicated to curriculum enrichment. You may well find that your local university will be supportive of any efforts to smooth the post-16–HE transition and help design such a course. The Extended Project (level 2 or 3) also provides an outstanding opportunity to develop skills of independent learning, primary and/or secondary research and report-writing. Free-standing maths qualification (FSMQ) statistics can be used to enhance research methodology. More about that in the next chapter.

WHAT MAKES A COMPETENT AND EFFECTIVE PSYCHOLOGY TEACHER?

This section begins with a call for critical thinking. We often use constructs like 'effectiveness' and 'competence' as if they had a reality independent of the current context. They do not. Currently, there is a trend in quality assurance and performance management for defining effectiveness by student attainment, not even taking account of value-added measures let alone a holistic view of education. Yet education is multifaceted. Who is really more effective, the teacher who maintains the straight A-grades their cohort arrived with or the teacher who moves students from a low starting point to a middling outcome? Who is really more effective, the teacher who gets excellent exam results, the teacher whose sensitivity prevents a suicide or the teacher who inspires the next Loftus or Baron-Cohen? These are, of course, daft questions – all the above are great achievements – but they serve a serious purpose in highlighting the difficulty in pinning down real quality teaching without locating it in a particular context.

■ **Box 1.1 Strategies to better prepare post-16 students for a psychology degree**

■ Get students used to using electronic resources. Psychology undergraduates will use library databases to locate books, specialised databases like PsycINFO to find original studies and statistical packages like SPSS to analyse data. Much of this software is beyond school and college budgets but there are similar and very user-friendly free and open source packages with which psychology students can become familiar (see Chapter 7 for details).

■ Expose students to a range of texts that represent the same material differently and which express contrasting views. Part of the 'acculturation' that concerns some HE teachers occurs because at school and college level it is possible for students to think of what is in their textbook as 'fact'. At undergraduate level they will have to recognise that each textbook contains merely a representation of the original material presented and evaluated in the light of the author's interpretation and biases.

■ There are other ways to encourage students to think beyond textbook contents. Doug Bernstein, former Chair of the National Institute for the Teaching of Psychology, has pioneered a useful exercise in which he gives groups of students the task of summarising studies described in his textbooks and showing students how different their interpretations of the study are to his own and to each other's (Bernstein, personal communication).

■ Expose students to some psychology journals. Although journal papers are initially intimidating to anyone, mostly because of the statistical analyses, it is possible with appropriate scaffolding for students to extract much more detailed information about studies from original papers than from textbook accounts of them. A useful exercise is to present students papers with abstracts removed with – carefully selected for conceptual level – and have students generate their own abstracts.

■ Focus on teaching psychological thinking throughout the course. For example, rather than teach evaluation points for theories and studies, focus on teaching how to evaluate theories and studies. This develops the transferable skill of critical thinking. Strategies to achieve this are discussed in Chapter 4.

■ Expose students to academic psychologists. Many lecturers are happy to give talks in schools and colleges. Remember, as well, that academics are often short of research participants, and that your students can gain valuable experience of seeing 'real' research in action by serving as participants. See Chapter 3 for a model of how this has been achieved.

Operationalising competence

Competent teaching is currently operationalised by means of a set of standards, available at a range of levels, starting with the Q (qualification) standards needed to pass a PGCE course, and divided into three categories:

■ Professional attributes
■ Professional knowledge and understanding
■ Professional skills.

Measures of effectiveness and competence can be useful in reflecting on professional development, and the current competency standards are certainly thorough and wide ranging. Effectiveness and competency are, however, just social constructs and not absolutes. Problems begin when we start to assume that all these criteria are sufficiently all embracing and robust to make valid judgements about teachers, and when we start to ignore achievements that don't neatly fit into the frameworks.

The concept of good practice

Any rant about ideas like effectiveness and competence would be incomplete without a mention of 'good practice'. Most of us have innocently used this term when recommending a technique or strategy. However, it can have sinister connotations. In a recent paper, Coffield and Edward (2009) have attacked the rolling out of 'good', 'best' and 'excellent' practice, comparing the progression through these terms to a 'ratchet screwdriver with no reverse movement allowed' (2009: 373). As Rice and Brooks said of best practice: 'Even if the judgement is backed by an appropriate theoretical background and teaching experience, it remains a judgement and one likely to be challenged by the next professional with similar background and experience' (2004: 86). The term 'best' causes particular problems because it implies that there is a single best way of doing things, regardless of the situation. This is unlikely to be true, and psychology teachers are in a good position to challenge the evidence on which bold assertions of 'best practice' are made. This is important in maintaining teachers' professional autonomy (Jarvis, 2010).

A values-led alternative

After working with the current limited notions of effectiveness and the thorough but rather rigid and mechanistic competency framework it can be refreshing to look at literature from abroad. Perlman and McCann (1999) offer a framework for psychology teachers based more on positive values than competencies:

■ To get students the highest grade possible
■ To teach students about the subject matter of psychology
■ To enthuse students about psychology
■ To teach students to think like psychologists
■ To use psychology to teach generic skills
■ To use psychology to understand the world.

This range of aims reflects a (healthy) tension between academic excellence, idealism and pragmatism. We can extract from the Perlman and McCann a simple tripartite model of the characteristics of the effective psychology teacher:

■ Subject knowledge and skills – including research design and critical thinking

■ Generic and subject-specific teaching skills – the latter including, for example, running practicals and teaching psychological thinking
■ Assessment regime expertise.

Subject knowledge and skills

It is a truism that effective teaching requires a minimum level of subject knowledge. This includes knowledge of both the subject and the skills that go with it, for example, research design and critical thinking. What is much less clear is the extent to which good teaching is associated with subject expertise beyond this minimum. The reality on the ground has always been that some teachers will be professionally qualified psychologists while others will be just a few pages ahead of their students in a textbook. A number of small-scale surveys have looked at exactly how many psychology teachers have psychology qualifications.

In a survey for the British Psychological Society (Jarvis, 2003), a substantial minority of psychology teachers – 28% of school teachers and 19% of further education (FE) lecturers – did not have an HE qualification in the subject. More recently Rowley and Dalgarno (2010) found a similar number of school teachers without a psychology degree (28.6%), but a smaller number of FE lecturers, just 2.5%. All such surveys have problems with sample size and representativeness so don't take the exact percentages as gospel. Suffice to say that a substantial minority of psychology teachers have no formal qualifications in psychology. This is absolutely not to suggest that psychology teachers without a psychology background cannot be good psychology teachers. It does however highlight a direction for continuous professional development (CPD) – 100% of Jarvis' sample who did not have psychology degrees reported that they would undertake a suitable qualification in psychology if it existed.

Generic and subject-specific teaching skills

Shulman (1986) made the important distinction between pedagogy and subject-pedagogy; in other words there exist generic teaching attributes, knowledge and skills, but also more subject-specific ways of doing things. This is important because the 33 competences currently applied to teachers are entirely generic. One weakness of the competency framework is that it does not easily recognise the creativity and specific expertise employed by teachers in delivering their own subject. On reading this book it should become clear that, while generic teaching skills are important, there are in addition a number of subject-specific techniques developed for psychology teaching. Some of these have not been widely disseminated among psychology teachers and they represent an important direction for professional development in experienced teachers. Examples include Sternberg's triarchic model of psychology teaching (p86), Dietz-Uhler and Lanter's four-question model (p88), Norton's use of PALS (p48) and McGhee's thinking skills toolkits (p81).

Assessment regime expertise

This refers not to the generic skill of assessing student progress during courses, but specifically to the understanding teachers need to develop of the processes by which the outcomes of their courses will be assessed. For most psychology teachers this will mean understanding the assessment procedures followed by the unitary awarding bodies responsible for psychology GCSE and A-level. Some of these are discussed further in Chapter 2, and a number of training providers – including the exam boards themselves, learned bodies such as the Association for the Teaching of Psychology and private training companies – provide workshops on A-level teaching and marking. However, there is no substitute for first-hand experience, and the best way to gain an in-depth understanding of the exam system is probably to become an assistant examiner. Most teachers report after their first experience of examining that they have a better understanding of how to prepare students for exams and some rethink much of their practice. Paradoxically this is at least as important if you have a holistic view of education. The better you understand the exam system the more efficiently you can prepare students for it and the more time you can free for other activities.

PROFESSIONAL VISIONS OF THE PSYCHOLOGY TEACHER

If we have established a range of goals of psychology teaching and explored some of the attributes of the psychology teacher that contribute to their achievement, perhaps the next logical task is to look at how the psychology teacher can achieve those attributes. Two models are of particular interest, reflecting the dual professional identity of the psychology teacher. The reflective professional model has been particularly influential in education. The scientist-practitioner model dominates applied psychology.

The reflective professional

For a more detailed account of reflectivity see Jarvis (2005). What follows here is a condensed version of that discussion. A broad vision widely espoused by educationalists has been of the teacher as a 'reflective professional'. The term captures effectively the essence of teaching as having professional status and the teacher as an active participant in both individual professional development and as a contributor to wider pedagogical development.

The most influential view of reflective practice comes from Schon (1983, 1987). Schon has put together a complex model of professional expertise by fusing cognitive and social constructionist theory. Based on social constructionist awareness, Schon proposed that professions entered a crisis by the 1980s due to the growing awareness of the limitations of technical rationality, the dominant belief that professional ability could be understood simply in terms of mastering a set of skills. Based on a cognitive understanding of automatic processing of information

(Allport, 1980; Tharp and Gallimore, 1991), Schon developed the term 'knowledge in action' to describe the ability of the experienced professional to respond automatically to a situation without diverting attentional resources and distraction. Rather than subscribing to technical rationality, Schon suggested that professional expertise could be better understood in terms of 'professional artistry', whereby experienced professionals make use of knowledge in action.

To Schon the reflective professional is distinguished by the capacity to consciously bring to bear a subjective awareness of their knowledge in action. This means that actions that would otherwise be implicit and automatic become explicit and can be reflected upon individually and shared in a process of professional discourse. Much of this reflection occurs simultaneously with the action, thus the reflective professional is constantly analysing and modifying their practice. This is called reflection in action. This is not, as has been sometimes suggested, to devalue the automatic processing involved in responding to situations in the form of teachers' craft knowledge, but rather to suggest that conscious reflection upon these automatic processes is an effective tool of professional development.

Schon's ideas have been enormously influential in educational academia. The concept of reflectivity has enormous heuristic value – that is, as a cognitive tool to aid thinking about a topic – among those seeking to look at development of pedagogy. Among practitioners, the term 'reflective practice' has also proved something of a rallying cry for those seeking to improve the professional status of teachers and been linked closely with Schon. This is not to say that Schon is without critics. Usher *et al.* (1997) have pointed out a logical inconsistency between reflection in action as a feature of professional practice and deliberate attempts to apply Schon's model by demonstrating reflectivity. Those influenced by Schon can only try to apply the model and, by definition, this cannot achieve Schon's ideal. In addition, Schon's liberal mix of cognitive and social constructionist principles is epistemologically messy, fusing theoretical ideas based upon largely incompatible views of the nature of knowledge and human understanding.

Evidence-based practice: the psychology teacher as scientist practitioner?

If reflectivity has been the dominant idea in understanding the teacher as professional, then the professions of applied psychology have been similarly dominated by the scientist-practitioner ethos. Essentially this means that the psychologist is both a practitioner and researcher, and that the practising psychologist contributes to research and tries as far as possible to use techniques that have been validated by research. The British Psychological Society's Division for Teachers and Researchers in Psychology (DTRP) promotes the ideal of linking teaching and research in its stated aims 'to ensure that the essential mutual relationships between teaching and research – so special within psychology – are sustained wherever psychologists are engaged in teaching; and to promote the application of psychological knowledge in the settings where psychological research is conducted and psychology is taught' (British Psychological Society, 1997).

There are serious problems in attempting to crudely emulate the scientist-practitioner ethos as it applies to other areas of applied psychology. One problem – felt even in clinical practice where the role of psychologist is distinguished from other therapeutic professionals by the science–practice link – is that the scientist-practitioner label can seem precious and elitist (Shapiro, 2002). This could present considerable problems for psychology teachers in the face of the egalitarian ethos of the staffroom. Moreover, evidence-based practice is currently made difficult by the small volume of directly relevant good quality research. Although the quality and relevance of education research has vastly improved over the last decade – at least from the perspective of empirical psychology – it still has a way to go before it bears comparison with medicine or clinical psychology (Torgerson *et al.*, 2005).

Clearly then, neither the state of the evidence base nor the context in which psychology teachers operate is conducive to adopting a strict scientist-practitioner ethos. However, there is no reason why teaching should not be informed by research provided teachers have realistic expectations and retain a sense of ownership of their practice. The more politically neutral term 'research informed psychology teaching' is now used to gently promote the influence of empirically validated technique (Zinkiewicz *et al.*, 2003). Actually there are some compelling reasons for psychology teachers to at least dip into the research literature of psychology teaching and to consider contributing to that literature.

1   Accounts of techniques used successfully elsewhere can inspire teachers broaden their own professional understanding and practice. This is true even when research has been conducted in a different context, for example US schools or universities in the United Kingdom. This is not to suggest that teachers should make knee-jerk responses and change their teaching to follow evidence-based practices, just that perusing research can inspire innovation.

2   In the current era of accountability teachers have increasingly to justify their practice (Guskey, 2007). Being able to refer to published evidence is a powerful argument for doing things your way. This is especially the case when you can demonstrate personal expertise by means of citing your own publications.

3   The term 'evidence-based practice' is being spoken with increasing frequency in government circles in relation to education. In the light of the growing expectation that teaching methods will conform to the empirically verified, there is a real danger that teacher discretion and hence professional status will be eroded. Top-down direction of teaching methods was explicit in both New Labour (Rammel and Haysom, 2006) and Tory (Gove, 2010) policy. Such control can only be resisted if teachers actively contribute to the evidence base, demonstrating that, in fact, they 'know best'. Psychotherapists, a decade

or so ahead of teachers in facing this issue, have responded by supplementing the top-down evidence-based practice agenda with a bottom-up agenda of practice-based evidence (Barkham and Mellor-Clark, 2000).

4   Researching your own practice is likely to lead to an enhanced understanding of what happens in your classroom. Psychology teachers, with a degree of disciplinary knowledge of research methods, are well placed to research their own practice. Moreover, as Nummedal *et al.* (2002) point out, consideration of what happens in teaching and learning should be intrinsically interesting to proponents of psychology – a discipline largely devoted to establishing cause and effect relationships. More pragmatically, conducting this type of research is recognised as continuing professional development and can form part of performance management.

5   While the current evidence base for psychology teaching is limited, we can work towards a more substantial body of evidence and cautiously begin to identify techniques that can be said to be reliably demonstrated to work in the context in which psychology teachers work. For example, a technique demonstrated to work well in an American university department of sociology *may* prove effective in the psychology A-level classroom of the UK school. If we ignore it on the basis of the context in which it originated, we may be missing a trick. Clearly though we cannot take it as read that the same technique will benefit practice in our very different context. The logical way to respond to such a technique would be to replicate and evaluate it in the psychology classrooms of UK schools and colleges.

At the time of writing there are two UK research journals looking to publish papers on practice in teaching psychology at school and college. These are *Psychology Teaching Review*, published by the British Psychological Society, and the *e-Journal of Psychology Teaching*, published by the Psychology Teacher Training Network.

Applying psychology to teaching psychology

This can be considered as an aspect of evidence-based practice in the wider sense that we can apply an empirically validated psychological theory to teaching psychology, even when such theory may not have been validated specifically in the context of teaching psychology. Zinkiewicz *et al.* (2003) have suggested a range of ways in which disciplinary knowledge of psychology can be applied to teaching psychology. These are summarised in Table 1.4.

Clearly the application of psychology to teaching psychology is tremendously broad and we cannot do justice to it in this short section. Many of the areas identified by Zinkiewicz and colleagues form the basis of discussions in this book. For those particularly interested in developing this area of their practice there are now Master's degrees in psychology teaching.

■ **Table 1.4** Examples of applying psychology to teaching psychology (After Zinkiewicz *et al.*, 2003)

Area of psychology	Examples of applicable theory and research
Cognitive development	Piaget's genetic epistemology, Vygotsky's sociocultural theory and research into adult cognitive development
Student diversity	Intelligence and ability, personality, learning styles, cultural diversity
Learning and thinking	Behavioural theory, experiential theory, cognitive approaches, theories of memory and learning
Motivation	Intrinsic and extrinsic motives, humanistic theories, cognitive theories
Social processes	Group development, conformity, intergroup relations, attitude change and leadership
Barriers to and facilitators of learning	Arousal, anxiety and stress Psychotherapy and resilience

CONCLUSIONS AND REFLECTIONS

Students overwhelmingly opt to study psychology because it fits neatly with our current cultural understanding of what is intrinsically interesting. There is little empirical support for alternative explanations for psychology's increasing popularity. As well as a qualification, students studying psychology have the opportunity to gain a set of transferable skills and a possible advantage in studying psychology at degree level. However, neither of these benefits should be taken for granted, and it is important that teachers are aware of making the subject interesting and engendering transferable skills. Two visions of the professional are particularly important in understanding how psychology teachers can develop their practice. The reflective professional model is particularly influential in teaching, while the scientist-practitioner model is similarly influential in psychology. While both of these models have their limitations, they are helpful in pointing to directions for continuing professional development.

An issue that has arisen continually through this chapter is the balance between two philosophies of teaching: that which emphasises exam success alone and that which focuses as much on quality of student experience and development of student attributes and transferable skills. Although there is no argument to be made that results are not important, teachers do vary in their attitudes to the relative value of student grades as compared to other criteria. Crudely, we can identify a continuum between what we might call strategic teaching on one hand – oriented purely towards maximising exam results – and holistic teaching on the other – balancing exam preparation against the quality of student experience and the achievement of more distal goals.

Although this is one of the most talked-about issues among psychology teachers it has generated surprisingly little literature. Drawing on his experience as HE teacher and A-level Chief Examiner, Green (2007) has denounced what he calls the 'cookbook approach' to psychology teaching: delivering formulaic chunks of information that allow students to technically satisfy assessment criteria without giving students a genuine understanding of the material. The question then arises: is the problem an over-emphasis on strategic teaching or the pedagogically poor approach that some teachers have taken to achieve it? In a context where teachers are constrained by the focus on them in terms of student attainment there is probably more to be gained by a focus on the latter. The philosophy of the rest of this book is about searching for a set of strategies and techniques that are compatible with an exam focus in the short term and also with the development of transferable skills in the long term.

QUESTIONS FOR REFLECTION

1   Critically consider the reasons why students choose psychology. What implications do these reasons have for professional practice?
2   To what extent does studying psychology help students beyond their course? What can teachers do to influence the long-term benefits of studying psychology?
3   What is effectiveness and what makes a psychology teacher effective?
4   What are the benefits of research-informed psychology teaching?
5   Outline the range of ways in which psychology has been applied to teaching psychology.

NOTE

1   A copy of the Dearing Report can be found at https://bei.leeds.ac.uk/Partners/NCIHE/

FURTHER READING

Jarvis, M. (2005) *The psychology of effective learning and teaching*. Cheltenham, Nelson Thornes.

McGuinness, C. (ed) (2003) *Post-16 qualifications in psychology*. Leicester, British Psychological Society.

Zinkiewicz, L., Hammond, N., and Trapp, A. (2003) *Applying psychology disciplinary knowledge to psychology teaching and learning*. York, LTSN.

CHAPTER 2

UNDERSTANDING THE PSYCHOLOGY CURRICULUM

By the end of this chapter you should be able to:

- Be aware of and explain the recent growth in the popularity of psychology.
- Outline the core elements of the psychology curriculum as outlined by QCDA.
- Compare the coverage of these elements in the five A-level and four GCSE specifications, and be aware of some criteria that might affect your choice of specification.
- Consider the importance of assessment objectives (AOs) in teaching and assessing psychology.
- Be aware of additional qualifications in psychology including Access to HE and SQA Higher.
- Discuss the rigour of psychology A-level in comparison to other subjects.
- Understand the role of benchmarking in assessing department performance and how to obtain and use appropriate benchmarks.

In the past two decades, psychology at a range of levels has grown at an unprecedented rate. In particular, A-level numbers have increased by up to 20% a year. The main purpose of this chapter is to better understand the psychology curriculum. There is a particular focus in this chapter on psychology A-level simply because the numbers of students taking A-level have been so much higher than for other qualifications, and therefore most debates about the curriculum have focused on A-level.

The Qualifications and Curriculum Development Authority (QCDA) has laid down a set of core elements to psychology at GCSE and A-level. However these are broad and open to interpretation. This has meant that, in contrast to some subjects where specifications from different awarding bodies are almost indistinguishable, there is a very healthy contrast between the content and approaches of the five psychology A-level and four GCSE specifications currently available. I say 'healthy' because this diversity allows psychology teachers an opportunity to exercise a degree of professional discretion in choosing the specification that best meets their abilities and the needs of their students. In fairness, we should acknowledge that the lack of commonality of experience in students going on to undergraduate study causes problems for both students and teachers in higher education (HE) (see Chapter 1 for a discussion). It would be inappropriate in a book like this to attempt to influence teachers' choices of specification, but it is worth briefly examining specifications and discussing the criteria that might affect your decisions.

A second aim of this chapter is to look at some current issues in the management of psychology curricula. One of these is the rigour of psychology – this is important in light of media coverage that suggests that 'newer' and 'trendy' subjects (psychology is certainly both of those) are easier than more traditional disciplines. Another is the assessment of psychology teachers and departments using benchmark data. Both of these are issues on which as psychology teachers you may be required to defend yourselves. This chapter may provide you with some ammunition with which to do this.

PSYCHOLOGY AS SCIENCE

To the bemusement of psychologists in HE, where psychology has long been recognised as a science, it is only since the run-up to Curriculum 2008 that psychology has shifted into the science domain as defined by QCDA. This creates a problem for curriculum developers in the sense that the sheer diversity of psychology makes it hard to look like the other sciences. Kimble (1999) and Conway (2007) have criticised the introductory psychology curriculum on the grounds that its very diversity fails to instil in students a shared scientific ethos. By contrast, Sternberg and Grigorenko (1999) have praised this breadth, pointing out that it reflects the nature of the discipline and that outstanding psychologists do not conform to a narrow set of standards. So what do psychology teachers think? Sutton (2006) reported a vigorous debate at a conference in the run-up to development of the 2008 A-level specification in which teachers appeared divided on the issue. However, surveying a larger and more representative group, Maras and Bradshaw (2007) asked teachers to respond to the statement 'psychology is a science'. Responses ranged from strongly disagree (scored as zero) to strongly agree (scored as 5). A mean of 3.8 emerged, with a small standard deviation, showing that in this sample teachers tended to agree that psychology was a science.

PSYCHOLOGY A-LEVEL

Numbers

The growth of A-level psychology over the past decade has been particularly remarkable. Numbers of AS and A-level candidates across the four awarding bodies and five specifications are shown in Table 2.1. By looking at AS numbers

■ **Table 2.1** Numbers of candidates completing psychology A-level (Source: awarding bodies)

Board/spec	AS numbers 2008	AS numbers 2009	AS numbers 2010	A2 numbers 2009	A2 numbers 2010
AQA spec A	47,841	40,262	48,608	31,697	31,739
AQA spec B	7,652	5,939	7,072	5,242	4,967
OCR	16,123	17,038	18,648	10,623	10,998
WJEC	2,158	5,892	6,446	1,410	3,795
Edexcel	6,810	3,888	5,652	4,211	3,741
Total (JCQ)	79,905	81,587	81,745	52,872	54,940

through 2008–10 and A2 numbers in 2009–10 it may be possible to identify some trends since the implementation of Curriculum 2008.

As we might expect, AQA Specification A, formerly the syllabus of AEB, being the oldest and best established of the syllabi still has the greatest market share. However, AQA A, along with Edexcel, took something of a hit in numbers with the changeover to Curriculum 2008. Although the overall numbers appeared to rise in 2009 this was actually an artefact of candidates resitting exams for the legacy specs. The number of students in the 2008–9 AS-level cohort fell for the first time in several years, although they picked up a little again in 2009–10. Anecdotal evidence suggests that there is significant teacher dissatisfaction with the new incarnations of more than one new specification and we can expect considerable movement between specifications over the next few years.

Factors affecting the growth of psychology

There is no single definitive answer as to why psychology has grown so much in popularity and there is currently little directly applicable empirical research. The following are offered as some likely factors.

■ *Growth of psychology-related careers*: Numbers of applied and academic psychologists are currently increasing. For example Lavender *et al.* (2003) report that since 1980 the number of training places in clinical psychology has increased by 309%. Numbers doubled between 1992 and 2002, making clinical psychology the fastest growing health profession. This means that, in contrast to previous 'glamour subjects' like sociology, psychology delivers on its promise of a clear progression pathway through first degree to a professional qualification as an applied psychologist.

■ *Changing cultural perceptions of scientific interest*: The increase in numbers of students opting for psychology has gone hand in hand with a decline in the numbers seeking to study traditional sciences, in particular physics and chemistry. A range of reasons has been suggested for this shift, including poor science teaching in schools and perceptions of traditional sciences as particularly difficult. However, one factor is certainly a perception of traditional sciences as 'dry' and lacking in intrinsic interest. Psychology by contrast is seen as of tremendous interest (Hirschler and Banyard, 2003; Walker, 2004).

■ *Glamorous media representations of psychology*: The most obvious example is Jimmy McGovern's *Cracker*, which ran from 1993–96. Since then it has become de rigueur for police dramas to feature a forensic or clinical psychologist. These psychologist characters are accorded tremendous status. When a forensic psychologist was criticised on *The Bill* by a cynical CID officer, a colleague expressed outrage: 'You can't talk about him like that … he's a Chartered Psychologist!' Popular literature has similarly become awash with hero-psychologists, notably Jonathan Kellerman's Alex Delaware and James Patterson's Alex Cross. As well as adding to the popular representation of psychology as intrinsically interesting, characters like these have provided role models for students to aspire to.

■ *The shift to four subject choices*: Prior to Curriculum 2000 it was standard practice to take three subjects at A-level. However, since 2000, the vast majority of AS-level students study four subjects. This has led to students being more adventurous in choosing a less familiar fourth subject. This has combined with the growth of public interest in psychology and perceptions of psychology as glamorous to boost its popularity.

These four suggestions, while difficult to test directly, are based on solid data, including growing numbers of applied psychologists, declining numbers of traditional scientists and increasing numbers of psychologists portrayed in glamorous roles in the media. Additional factors have been proposed but these are rather more speculative. For example, one suggestion is that the growth of psychology has gone hand in hand with a decline in church attendance, psychology providing a culturally appropriate secular belief system. Another is that increasing disillusion with the school curriculum is leading young people increasingly to opt for subjects, like psychology, which they have not studied previously.

Attainment

Tables 2.2a to 2.2c show AS-level grade distributions by awarding body for 2008 to 2010. 2008 was of course the last full year of the Curriculum 2000 specification whilst 2009 was the first year of the Curriculum 2008 spec.

A positive development appears to be a greater alignment in the grade distributions between the awarding bodies since 2009. This is critical because, if maintained, it should largely eliminate grade distribution as a factor in specification choice, giving teachers more freedom to choose a specification according to pedagogical rather than strategic criteria. Progression from AS to A2 may be another factor influencing specification choice (see Table 2.3).

■ **Table 2.2a** 2008 AS cumulative grade distribution by awarding body

	Total numbers	A (%)	B	C	D	E
JCQ combined	79,905	12.8	29.8	49.8	67.7	81.9
AQA A	47,841	12.2	28.2	47.5	65.3	79.8
AQA B	7,652	11.7	28.4	47.8	66.5	81.4
Edexcel	6,810	14.6	33.7	55.1	71.7	84.4
OCR	16,123	14.4	33.4	55.1	73.7	87.4
WJEC	2,158	13.0	28.6	48.3	67.1	80.9

■ **Table 2.2b** 2009 AS cumulative grade distribution by awarding body

	Total numbers	A (%)	B	C	D	E
JCQ combined (includes legacy)	81,587	12.6	29	48.9	67	81.5
AQA A	40,262	12.3	28.3	47.9	65.6	80.1
AQA B	5,939	11.1	26.7	46.4	64	78.9
Edexcel	3,888	10.9	26	45.2	62.9	78.2
OCR	17,038	10.9	25.1	43.75	63	78.5
WJEC	5,892	12.3	28.1	48.4	67	80.8

■ **Table 2.2c** 2010 AS cumulative grade distribution by awarding body

	Total numbers	A (%)	B	C	D	E
JCQ combined (includes legacy)	81,745	12.2	28.3	47.8	66.2	80.6
AQA A	48,608	12.7	29.1	49.0	67.4	81.5
AQA B	7,072	11.5	26.4	45.4	63.7	79.4
Edexcel	18,648	13.6	33.3	51.7	68.4	82.5
OCR	6,446	10.7	25.4	44.6	63.4	78.3
WJEC	5,652	12.1	28.0	46.5	65.9	80.5

We should of course be very cautious about reading too much into the comparisons between the progression rates of the different specifications as there are likely to be confounding demographic differences between the students studying each syllabus. One such demographic is gender, and it is clear that there are significant differences in the attainment of boys and girls. Table 2.4 shows attainment by boys and girls.

■ **Table 2.3** Progression from AS 2009 to A2 2010 (Source: awarding bodies)*

Board/spec	% progression to A2
AQA A	78.0%
AQA B	83.6%
OCR	64.5%
Edexcel	96.2%
WJEC	64.4%
overall	67.4%

* Progression rates are calculated by dividing 2010 A2 numbers by 2009 AS numbers. If candidates change awarding body between AS to A2 this will confound the figures, and these figures will be distorted in favour of awarding bodies (e.g. Edexcel) that allow transfers.

■ **Table 2.4** AS cumulative grade distribution by gender (Source: JCQ)

	Gender	A		B		C		D		E	
		2009	2008	2009	2008	2009	2008	2009	2008	2009	2008
Psychology	M	7.9	7.7	21.2	21.3	40.2	40.1	59.5	59.4	77.1	76
	F	14.8	15	32.6	33.5	53	53.8	70.6	71.1	83.4	84.3
All subjects	M	18.3	17.2	35.8	34.9	55.6	54.9	73.1	72.9	86.3	86.2
	F	20.5	19.9	40.9	40.2	61.5	61.6	78.3	78.6	89.9	89.1

It is clear from Table 2.4 that overall girls generally do better at A-level than boys. It can also be seen that this disparity was unchanged following the first year of Curriculum 2008. The picture in psychology is significantly worse. The disparity in male and female psychology results is considerably greater than the average disparity taken across all subjects, and it worsened significantly with the first round of awarding for Curriculum 2008.

A further development in recent years has been the movement of psychology into the school sector, psychology having being traditionally located in further education (FE) colleges. Most students of A-level psychology are now school-based. Only Edexcel publish figures by sector. Their psychology figures for 2009 are shown in Tables 2.5 and 2.6.

■ **Table 2.5** Proportions of psychology AS-level students in school and college sectors (Source: Edexcel)

% students in schools	% students in colleges	others
91.00%	7.50%	1.50%

■ **Table 2.6** Cumulative grade distributions in schools and colleges (Source: Edexcel)

Sector	A	B	C	D	E
School	11.4	27.2	46.8	64.1	79.1
FE	6.2	13.7	30.2	51.2	69.8

Although the available data are limited in extent it is clear that in raw attainment students do better in school 6th forms than in colleges – reflecting their higher typical entry grades, but perhaps also smaller class sizes.

The core psychology curriculum and A-level specifications

Based on the British Psychological Society's Qualifying Examination categories, the QCDA set out terms of reference on which the Curriculum 2000 and C2008 specifications were based. QCDA have specified that AS and A2 specifications were to include five broad areas:

- cognitive psychology
- biological psychology
- social Psychology
- developmental psychology
- the psychology of individual differences.

Research methodology is required in a psychology specification, but it can be a stand-alone or integrated into the rest of the content.

Prior to Curriculum 2000 there existed three psychology A-level syllabi, run by three of the four English exam boards, AEB, NEAB and Oxford & Cambridge. The boards were restructured into three Unitary Awarding Bodies, OCR (formerly Oxford & Cambridge), AQA (an amalgamation of AEB and NEAB) and Edexcel (formerly London Board). In 2000, OCR and AQA launched new specifications that, while conforming to the new QCA criteria, were designed to capture the essence of their pre-2000 A-level syllabi. At the same time, Edexcel launched a new psychology specification. In 2007, WJEC also entered the fray with an A-level specification. In spite of the common elements specified by QCA each of the current psychology specifications has a distinct content and character.[1]

Changes in Curriculum 2008

Curriculum 2000 arrived with a fanfare of publicity and elaborate teacher preparation while Curriculum 2008 seemed to slip in almost unannounced. Nonetheless Curriculum 2008 introduced some significant changes for psychology teachers. Most dramatically coursework was dropped, to mixed responses from teachers.

On one hand, designing, carrying out and writing up research undoubtedly fostered the development of a number of transferable skills (see p6 for a discussion). On the other hand, coursework was widely judged to have poor validity as an assessment method due to the potential for cheating and the fact that close adherence to slightly contrived mark schemes was at least as important in influencing grades as real quality of submission (Jarvis, 2006a).

Curriculum 2008 was designed to bring in additional changes. While Curriculum 2000 succeeded in its main goal of widening participation, the introduction of predominantly short-answer questions led to a widespread culture of shallow rote learning. Assessment in the Curriculum 2008 system has a greater emphasis on questions that require understanding as well as knowledge, for example by applying psychology to novel situations. Cutting from six to four units was meant to allow topics to be studied in greater depth.

The AQA A specification

This has the longest, best-established lineage among psychology A-levels. Until 2008 it was also perhaps the most traditional specification, however it now includes applied psychology. The current AS-level units are intended to cover the core areas of cognitive, developmental, biological, social psychology and individual differences. The A2 specification comprises a choice of topics from academic psychology and a choice of applied topic. In addition, all candidates study clinical psychology and research methods.

The AQA B specification

This is based on the second-oldest specification, and still maintains the distinctive character of the pre-2000 NEAB syllabus. The current AS-level units are intended to cover some key topics in social and cognitive psychology and individual differences, plus a general introduction to psychology including approaches and research methods. The A2 specification covers child development, a choice of applied topics and a final unit covering issues, debates and research methods.

The OCR specification

This is one of the younger specifications and arguably the most radical in approach. The emphasis at AS-level is on classic published studies – currently 15. In addition to the core studies, students are expected to be aware of theoretical approaches and undertake a unit of research methods. The A2 specification includes a choice of applied psychology topics, again with an emphasis on specified studies, and a unit covering issues and debates, approaches and research methods.

The Edexcel specification

This is a relatively new specification, having existed since 2000. The emphasis at AS-level is on theoretical perspectives, each including research methods and a choice of key studies and practicals. Currently Edexcel is alone in introducing inferential statistics at AS-level. At A2, candidates study a choice of applied psychology topics and a final unit covering clinical psychology, debates, approaches and research methods. A2 also includes content and article analyses designed to enhance transferable skills.

The WJEC specification

This is the newest specification, at AS-level taking an eclectic approach influenced by both the OCR core studies and Edexcel theoretical approaches models. Candidates study four approaches, each with a corresponding therapy, and 10 core studies. At A2 candidates take a unit in research methods and a further unit offering a choice of core topics, applications and controversies.

Assessment objectives

To fully understand the psychology curriculum and its assessment we need to be familiar not just with specification content but with assessment objectives. There are three assessment objectives (AOs) underlying the formal assessments made at AS and A2 level. They reflect different aspects of psychological thinking, discussed further in Chapter 4. For the first time in the C2008 specs there is a close convergence between the assessment objectives. The following are common to the four English specifications and similar to those in the WJEC spec. Much of the phrasing of these assessment objectives derives from the McGuinness report on developing thinking skills.

AO1

Candidates should be able to:

- recognise, recall and show understanding of scientific knowledge
- select, organise and communicate relevant information in a variety of forms.

AO2

Candidates should be able to:

- analyse and evaluate scientific knowledge and processes
- apply scientific knowledge and processes to unfamiliar situations including those related to issues
- assess the reliability, validity and credibility of scientific information.

AO3

Candidates should be able to:

■ describe ethical, safe and skilful practical techniques and processes, selecting appropriate qualitative and quantitative methods
■ know how to make, record and communicate reliable and valid observations and measurements with appropriate precision and accuracy, through using primary and secondary sources
■ analyse, interpret, explain and evaluate the methodology, results and impact of their own and others' experimental and investigative activities in a variety of ways.

OCR have added an additional AO2 point:

■ bring together scientific knowledge from different areas and apply them.

If you are not currently in the habit of building the assessment objectives into your planning you may be missing a trick. Exam questions are set according to the AOs, so assume that the sort of questions implied by the AOs will at some point be set. Past papers are a good guide to how the AOs might be assessed, but there is always pressure on principal examiners to address the AOs in novel ways.

GCSE PSYCHOLOGY

Numbers and attainment

Since the first edition of this book, GCSE psychology has taken off in a big way. For decades, psychology GCSE was almost exclusively the province of adult education and the nature of the specifications reflected this. When psychology was reclassified by QCDA as a science, qualification new specifications were written designed for the school curriculum. The new GCSE was launched in September 2009. At the time of writing the first cohort of students have just sat the GCSE exam. Although numbers and grade distributions are shown in Tables 2.7 and 2.8 respectively it is too soon to see emerging trends and these data should be viewed with caution.

■ **Table 2.7** Numbers completing GCSE psychology in 2010

Board	AQA	OCR
Numbers	4,204	4,910

■ **Table 2.8** 2010 grade distributions of GCSE psychology by awarding body

Board	A*	A	B	C	D	E	F	G
AQA	5.2	14.5	27.8	60.8	80.7	90.6	94.3	95.9
OCR	2.3	14.1	33.1	61.6	81.4	91.2	94.7	96.5

The core curriculum and the GCSE specifications

As for A-levels, the content of GCSE course is guided by the British Psychological Society's (BPS) qualifying examination. GCSE specs currently have two or three units, each assessed by means of an exam. Like A-level, GCSE psychology has recently lost its coursework element. Also like A-level, the four GCSE specifications each have their own distinct character, and each is congruent with its corresponding A-level. For example OCR has an emphasis on core studies while Edexcel integrates research methods with other topics.

The AQA specification

This covers a range of topics across the five BPS approaches, including memory, non-verbal communication, personality, prejudice, learning theory, social influence, sex and gender, and aggression. There are two units, with research methods being examined as separate topics in both exams.

The Edexcel specification

This two-unit specification is structured so that each topic includes a breakdown of the key research questions, including those related to perception, dreaming, video games, phobias and criminality. Methodology relevant to answering these and the practical applications of psychological knowledge are assessed with each topic.

The OCR specification

This differs from other psychology GCSEs in having three units, all assessed by exam. Units 1 and 2 each cover a topic from the five BPS approaches, for example, cognitive psychology is represented by perception and memory. Each topic includes a core study and practical applications. Unit 3 is a stand-alone research methods unit.

The WJEC specification

This is a two-unit specification, which maps directly on to the BPS approaches, with each approach being represented by three topics. For example, the biological approach is represented by stress, sensory organs and the brain. Research methodology is examined in unit 2 by means of a stand-alone question.

Assessment objectives

The GCSE assessment objectives are similar to those used at A-level, and the advice about using them for planning holds true here.

AO1

Students should be able to:

■ demonstrate knowledge and understanding of the psychological models, theories, explanations, concepts and terminology in the specification
■ show understanding of the relationship of psychological evidence with explanations and theories
■ show understanding of how psychological knowledge and ideas change over time and the evidence for these changes.

AO2

Students should be able to:

■ apply concepts, develop arguments and/or draw conclusions related to familiar and unfamiliar situations
■ show understanding and assess applications and uses of psychology with reference to contemporary situations
■ evaluate the impact of psychological findings, developments or processes on individuals and communities.

AO3: Interpretation, evaluation and analysis of psychological data and practice

Students should be able to:

■ plan a psychological investigation testing an idea, answering a question or solving a problem
■ show understanding of research methods and methodology in familiar and unfamiliar situations
■ evaluate methods and methodology used when collecting primary and secondary data, including ethical considerations
■ analyse and interpret qualitative and quantitative data from sources
■ discuss the validity and reliability of data in presenting and justifying conclusions.

CHOOSING A PSYCHOLOGY SPECIFICATION

If you are new to teaching psychology the chances are that you will not have been given any choice in which specification you teach to. However, your day-to-day experience as a psychology teacher will be significantly different according to which specifications your students are taking. It is instructive to at least be aware of the differences between the four GCSE and five A-level specifications, and, of course, you may find yourself in the position of having to choose in the future. If you are choosing a specification, be aware that it is a hugely important but far from straightforward task. All the specifications and their assessments have their loyalists and their detractors. This would not be the case if any of the five were perfectly suited to everyone, nor if any were entirely lacking in virtue. In that spirit – and to avoid lawsuits – rather than comment on the alleged strengths and weaknesses of each specification I offer a set of criteria to consider.

1   How interesting do you think your students will find the content? Given that the intrinsic sexiness of psychology is the most important factor in students' choice to study it in the first place, it is important to consider how interesting students will find the content of the specification you choose.

2   A related question concerns the extent to which each specification lends itself to interesting teaching methods. How, as well as what, you teach will impact on the quality of students' experiences. There is no consensus about which specification or specifications do this best; think about how you would be likely to deliver each specification and you may find that, for you personally, there are distinct winners and losers.

3   How do you perceive the discipline of psychology? Different specifications have different emphases on research methodology, studies, theory and application. Your personal emphasis will affect your perception of the educational value of each specification. If, for you, it is all about the studies, for example, some specifications are more closely aligned to your view than others.

4   Similarly, how applied do you think a psychology course should be? Different specifications have very different emphases on traditional academic and applied topics. If you're a traditionalist one specification might appeal most and if you're – in this sense – a moderniser, a different specification may appeal more.

5   What do you think constitutes good preparation for progression to psychology at the next level? Each GCSE specification has an approach congruent with the corresponding A-level specification, so there is a logic for sticking with one awarding body at the two levels. The five A-level specifications have varying degrees of similarity to the first-year undergraduate syllabus. You may believe that a similar or dissimilar A-level specification will be of greater benefit to students progressing to degree level. Alternatively you may not think this is an important criterion; it is about your personal philosophy.

6   Do different specifications provide differing levels of opportunity to develop

transferable skills in your students? You might want to consider differing emphases on essay-writing or differing opportunities to conduct primary research.

7   Alternatively, if you are more strategic in outlook, think about grade distributions and you may try to second guess which specification will most advantage your students in grade terms.

8   How transparent and appropriate do the assessment methods of each awarding body appear to you? Look at past exam papers and mark schemes or examiners' reports to get an idea of which Chief Examiner's thinking you are most in tune with.

9   What is the content-load of each syllabus? Look at both breadth and depth at this point – there is usually something of a trade-off so that specifications that appear shorter may require more depth of understanding. Think about the number of teaching hours you have available for each AS and A2 group. Look at how each specification would divide up week by week and consider how able your typical students are. You might favour one specification if you have small classes of highly selected students for six hours a week (yes there are still places that do that!) and a different one altogether if you see large groups of more mixed ability students for four hours a week.

OTHER PSYCHOLOGY QUALIFICATIONS

Access to HE

Access courses are tailor-made courses broadly equivalent in level to A-levels but designed to meet the needs of mature students returning to study and seeking to enter HE. They have existed for about 20 years. Courses generally include a range of subject options, psychology being a popular choice. Since 2002 Access courses have been kite-marked by the Quality Assurance Agency (the HE body approximately equivalent to QCDA). Courses are currently unitised under the Open College Network and units can either be written by teachers and accredited by an Open College Network or bought 'off the shelf'. Access units vary rather more than do A-level units because they have varying emphases on content and study skills development. Be aware of this when choosing or writing Access units – some courses are much more content-heavy than others. Statistics from HESA (the Higher Education Statistics Agency) are now dated but the last published comparison showed that Access students do roughly as well in degrees as do A-level students, with slightly fewer attaining first class and upper second class degrees but fewer failing.

SQA qualifications

Since 1999, The Scottish Qualifications Authority (SQA) has offered psychology at four of their five levels; Intermediate 1, Intermediate 2, Higher and Advanced

■ **Table 2.9** Degree classifications of Access students vs others (Source: Youell, 2003)

Entry qualification	1st	2:1	2:2	3rd/pass	Fail
Access	8.28%	41.98%	36.40%	9.40%	3.45%
Other	10.56%	45.41%	32.27%	7.18%	4.56%

Higher. The Higher has been regarded as the 'gold standard' for university entry and is roughly equivalent to AS-level. Levels 1, 2 and Higher consist of three mandatory units: understanding the individual (early socialisation, memory and stress); investigating behaviour (research methods); and the individual in social context (including social psychology – prejudice, anti-social behaviour, conformity and obedience relationships, and individual differences – intelligence and abnormality). The Advanced Higher (A2 equivalent) consists of two mandatory units – perspectives and research methods – and a choice of one of five specialisms in developmental, cognitive, social, biological psychology or individual differences. By 2009, 2,763 students took the Higher in psychology.

THE RIGOUR OF PSYCHOLOGY

With the tremendous growth in the numbers of students taking A-level psychology the subject has come under increasing scrutiny, and more conservative elements in the education establishment, notably John Dunford of the Association for School and College Leaders, have made highly disparaging comments about the rigour with which psychology A-level is assessed. Dunford's notorious assertion that psychology is easier than maths is reportedly based on a study by Fitz-Gibbon and Vincent (1994), which showed that students undertaking psychology A-level alongside more traditional subjects typically did better in psychology than in their other subjects and that, when GCSE profile was controlled for, students of psychology achieved better grades than students with comparable grades undertaking traditional subjects. This was a methodologically sound study, to be taken seriously if not accepted uncritically. However, the social and educational context in which A-levels are taken has changed considerably in the past two decades with a proportionate impact on the grade distribution across subjects (Morris, 2003). More recent data paint a rather more balanced picture. For example, data for A-levels taken in 2002 and 2008 from the Curriculum, Evaluation and Management Centre (CEM Centre) show that, when GCSE results are controlled for, the UCAS points achieved by students taking maths and psychology are very similar, both falling in the centre of the distribution of A-level subjects (see Figure 2.1). This suggests that psychology and maths are of comparable difficulty (Jarvis, 2004, in press).

CEM Centre data up to 2006 can be viewed free on the website www.cemcentre.org/attachments/Alis_A-Level%20Subject%20Difficulties.pdf

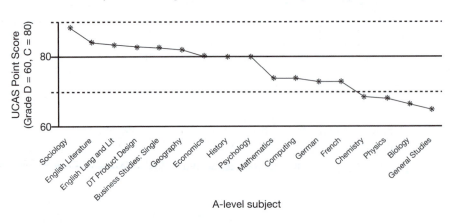

Expected A-level grade of student with average GCSE grade B

■ Figure 2.1 UCAS points achieved by students in 2002*

* Adapted from data from the CEM Centre

Psychology remained in the middle of the distribution of subject difficulty throughout the 1994–2006 period charted. Psychology teachers who enjoy a friendly rivalry with colleagues in sociology will enjoy the fact that by the CEM Centre criterion psychology emerged as significantly the more difficult of the two. It is also worth looking at grade distributions of different subjects. Table 2.10 takes AS grades as an example.

It is apparent from Table 2.10 that psychology A-level has a relatively low A–E and A–C pass rate in relation to some more traditional subjects, suggesting that it is in fact relatively difficult. Further evidence to support the rigour of psychology A-level comes from student surveys, which suggest that psychology is typically perceived as at least as difficult as respondents' other subjects. Hirschler and Banyard (2003) surveyed 454 post-16 psychology students – 92% of whom were studying AS/A-level – about their perceptions of the difficulty of psychology. Table 2.11 shows the percentages of respondents believing psychology to be easier, equivalent to or more difficult than other subjects.

■ Table 2.10 AS-level grade distributions by subject 2009 (Source: JCQ)

	A	B	C	D	E
Psychology	12.60%	29.00%	48.90%	67.00%	76.90%
Sociology	16.20%	34.60%	55.60%	73.30%	86.20%
Biology	18.60%	35.10%	53.30%	69.40%	82.60%
Chemistry	22.20%	40.20%	57.30%	72.60%	85.30%
Maths	30.80%	47.20%	61.70%	74.20%	84.30%
All subjects	18.30%	35.80%	55.60%	73.10%	86.30%

■ **Table 2.11** Student perceptions of the difficulty of psychology (Adapted from Hirschler and Banyard, 2003)

Level of difficulty	% of respondents
Psychology more difficult	43
Psychology equally difficult	30
Psychology less difficult	27

In this sample, the modal response was that psychology was perceived as more demanding than the subjects taken alongside it. Responses were similar when students were questioned regarding the workload in psychology and their other subjects. None of the above sets of data in isolation show conclusively that psychology is rigorous. However, taken together they paint a convincing picture. Don't let the traditionalists bully you.

The 'dumbing down' argument

A final criticism that can be countered by statistical evidence concerns the general 'dumbing down' of A-level exams. This is a common criticism as A-levels have adapted to an agenda of widening participation. Given that general cognitive ability is normally distributed throughout the population and that a much wider spectrum of candidates are undertaking advanced-level study this is a legitimate research question (Rust and Golombok, 1999). However, it is essential that the importance of an issue does not lead us to prejudge the outcome. It may be that changes to A-levels have been qualitative rather than quantitative, reflecting greater transparency and a reduction in bias towards the cultural capital of middle class students. In any case the dumbing-down argument is based on the assumption that as the number of candidates increases so does the proportion of low ability candidates. This is an entirely inappropriate basis on which to challenge psychology A-level given that, whereas until about 10 years ago psychology was predominantly offered in FE colleges, it is now an important part of the 6th form curriculum, where standards are typically higher (Morris, 2003).

Using benchmark information

It is now standard quality assurance practice to compare psychology departments in schools and colleges against national benchmarks. Value-added data are also available, and the value of raw versus value-added data is the subject of much debate. At the time of writing the pendulum is swinging towards a new emphasis on raw data.

While it is inherently tempting to see 'how one is doing' by looking at this type of data, by virtue of our disciplinary knowledge psychology teachers are in a position to look more critically at the data we are judged against. It is tempting to see a benchmark as a gold standard against which we must fare well. However, there are a number of ways of obtaining benchmark figures, and benchmarks can vary considerably according to their origins. When presented with a benchmark figure, critically consider it in the light of the following:

■ Is the figure you are given up-to-date? There are some year-on-year variations in grade distributions, and although trends are generally upwards this has not been true every year for all psychology specifications.

■ Does the figure you are given refer to the specification you take? In some years there are substantial variations in the grade distributions across different specifications. Anecdotal evidence suggests that purveyors of value-added systems do not necessarily take account of these variations and this can leave you at a disadvantage.

■ Does the figure you are given refer to your sector? There is some variation between schools and colleges, particularly in A–C rates. If you work in an FE college check that your benchmark figures are not derived from school 6th forms, which typically have higher attainment.

■ Do you have separate benchmark figures for male and female achievement, or is the figure you receive adjusted for the proportion of male and female students you teach? Girls' achievements outstrip those of boys in psychology to a much greater extent than in most subjects,[2] so if you have a higher percentage of boys than the national average for your specification and this is not taken into account in any analysis of your performance you may be seriously disadvantaged.

The quality of benchmarks supplied to schools and colleges is increasing. However it cannot necessarily be relied on. Accurate benchmark information, referring to your specification, and showing male and female norms, can be obtained from the websites of the awarding bodies.

CONCLUSIONS AND REFLECTIONS

Psychology at post-16 level, in particular A-level, has grown at an unprecedented rate in the past five years. Factors affecting this probably include the shift in cultural norms of intrinsic interest and the resulting glamorous media representations of psychologists. This represents a great opportunity for psychology teachers but also a challenge; students expect a lot from us, and it is important in choosing specifications, resources and teaching methods that we try to meet these expectations.

GCSE and A-level psychology specifications are now written to a set of core criteria laid down by QCA, and are examined on a common set of assessment objectives. However, the five A-level specifications each have a distinct character of their own. All the specifications have loyal supporters, so check them out for yourself and don't rely on past practice or the preference of a non-specialist such as your Head Teacher. The criteria for choosing a specification are personal, relating to teachers' perceptions of the fit between each specification and their beliefs about psychology and their intuitive understanding of the thinking of the examiners. There isn't an overall 'best' specification but there is probably one that best suits you and your students.

There have been questions asked about the rigour with which 'newer' and fashionable subjects are assessed at post-16 level. In the case of psychology, data from a number of sources, including UCAS points of students undertaking different subjects, grade distributions and student perceptions, suggest that psychology is rigorously assessed. Another issue facing psychology teachers concerns benchmark data. Be aware of the variable quality of benchmarks available and be sure that you obtain the up-to-date figures that pertain to your specification and sector.

QUESTIONS FOR REFLECTION

1　How and why has psychology grown so much in popularity as a post-16 subject?

2　Outline the core psychology curriculum and explain how this is interpreted differently in the GCSE and A-level specifications.

3　How might a teacher choose between the four GCSE or five A-level specifications?

4　What evidence is there to support psychology A-level as a rigorously assessed A-level?

5　How can you be sure you are comparing your success rates against the correct benchmarks?

NOTES

1　The specifications can be downloaded in full from the awarding body websites. Web addresses are provided in Appendix II.

2　See Chapter 7 for a detailed discussion of gender and achievement.

FURTHER READING

Jarvis, M. (2004) The rigour and appeal of psychology A-level. *Education Today* **54**, 24–8.
http://www.qcda.gov.uk/curriculum/secondary/552.aspx

CHAPTER 3

FOUR PRINCIPLES OF EFFECTIVE LEARNING AND TEACHING

By the end of this chapter you should be able to:

■ Be aware of some of the principles believed to underlie effective learning and teaching.
■ Understand the constructivist perspective and the importance of active learning, with particular regard to enquiry-based, problem-based and multiple-perspective teaching.
■ Understand some principles of social constructivist education and use social constructivist principles to develop interactivity in learning, with particular regard to collaborative learning and peer tutoring.
■ Appreciate the importance of making psychological material relevant to students, for example by means of Psychology Applied Learning Scenarios (PALS) and experiential learning.
■ Outline some principles of information-processing theory and discuss the importance of structuring material and practising recall by means of tests and quizzes.
■ Discuss the use of metacognitive strategies for exam preparation.

Teaching is important. And that isn't just a statement of the bleeding obvious. Over the past decade considerable research has gone into trying to untangle the effects of school quality, teaching quality, learner demographics, learner motivation and prior learning on both proximal outcomes in the form of attainment and more distal outcomes such as performance at university. Broadly there is a consensus in published reviews that the quality of teaching has a major impact on students' attainment (Rivkin *et al.*, 2005; Eide *et al.*, 2004; Naylor and Smith, 2002). Perhaps more controversially, there is also some evidence to suggest that the impact of highly strategic teachers in schools that we might call 'exam factories' is temporary (Naylor and Smith, 2002). In other words, students who have been drilled for exams without developing transferable skills can do well at GCSE and A-level but are likely to underachieve at university. There is therefore a sound empirical reason as well as an ideological one to look for ways of teaching that maximise 'real' or 'deep' learning and develop transferable skills, as well as equip students to cope with their assessment regime.

We have all heard about the 'correct' or 'best' way to teach. It is crucial to separate out the idea that quality of teaching is important from the idea that it is important to teach in a particular way. Those who have been around a while will have heard a number of rather different takes on what constitutes 'the correct way to teach'. Since the New Labour years, governments have taken the lead on isolating and sharing the characteristics of effective teaching (Rammel and Haysom, 2006; Gove, 2010). Psychology teachers, with a foot in the camps of psychology and education, are well placed to see the positives and downsides of this. On one hand, as scientists we can see the potential benefits of evidence-based practice. On the other hand, as practitioners we are often more sensitive than researchers to the limitations of generalising research findings to a range of different contexts. While the sharing of good pedagogical practice has encouraged healthy debate and innovation, real consensus has proved elusive, and fashions in teaching can still change rapidly. In any case, there is always a complex interaction between teaching strategies and the characteristics of the individual teacher, the topic and students, both as individuals and groups. This means that while there may be a best way for one teacher to teach a particular topic to a particular class on a particular day (unfortunately this usually becomes more obvious after the lesson!) we would be very unwise to say that there is a single best approach to teaching psychology as a whole.

Bearing all that in mind, the aim of this chapter is not to prescribe a particular model of teaching. Nor is it even to suggest that good teaching is primarily a matter of implementing a set of techniques – research has shown clearly that students rate the quality of their relationship with their teacher as more important than their choice of pedagogical techniques (Jarvis, 2005). The much more modest aim of this chapter is to present a range of psychological principles and lines of research and practice in the belief that all teachers, however experienced and competent, might benefit from considering both the rationale underlying what they already do and the possibility of extending their current practice.

Without favouring a particular approach to teaching, it is possible to cautiously attempt to draw from the range of contemporary theory and research a set of basic principles that can be said to underlie effective learning and teaching. There are perhaps six such principles that we can say are important in affecting the quality of teaching and learning.

1   Learning should be an active process. High levels of student involvement can be achieved in a variety of activities, including whole-class, small group and independent exercises. It is a common misunderstanding that students are only active if they are working without input from a teacher.

2   Learning can be enhanced by appropriate social interaction. This interaction can be with a teacher or with peers, or even with software, can be in-person or remote and can take place in a range of whole-class, small group or individual but technologically connected exercises.

3   Students are likely to be most actively involved in their learning when the subject matter is inherently relevant to them or made so by teaching. Thus teaching should involve applying research and theory to real-life scenarios.

4   Learning needs to be well remembered. However much emphasis we place on the distal purposes of teaching, such as developing transferable skills and preparation for studying psychology at higher levels, there is a proximal aim to prepare students for assessment, which is primarily by means of exams.

5   Learning is as much about developing skills, including more advanced ways of thinking, as it is about mastering a set of facts.

6   Teaching must take account of the diverse needs of learners.

Developing psychological thinking and catering for student diversity warrant their own chapters. The remainder of this chapter is devoted to applying psychological theory and research to developing the first four principles in teaching psychology.

MAKING LEARNING ACTIVE: THE CONSTRUCTIVIST POSITION

The constructivist tradition owes much to the ideas of Jean Piaget, but is inextricably linked to the ideas of other pioneers such as John Dewey. To psychology teachers, Piaget will forever be inextricably linked to a stage model of cognitive development. However, Piaget's work was much broader than this, suggesting a distinctive approach to understanding learning. Piaget put great emphasis on human curiosity and saw learning as an active motivated process in which we constantly construct successively more complex understandings of the world. The concept that perhaps distinguishes Piaget's view of learning from alternative approaches is agency. To Piaget 'agency' referred to the human motivation to actively pursue knowledge; in other words to be the agents of our own learning. This active learning is stimulated by a state of disequilibrium or perturbation, the uncomfortable sensation of not understanding a situation. As we pursue knowledge of a topic, we construct successively more advanced mental representations of it – hence the term 'constructivist.'

Although it is possible for students to be fully engaged in active learning in whole-class activity, for example when discussing or debating an issue, the emphasis in constructivist education has been on shifting practice away from whole-class didactic teaching, in which the teacher takes the active role and students a generally more passive role, towards student-centred activity in which learners pursue topics independently. Sizer puts it thus: 'The governing practical metaphor of the school should be student-as-worker rather than the more familiar teacher-as-deliverer-of-instructional-services' (1992: 226).

To put it simply, constructivist lessons involve students finding or working things out for themselves – what we might call 'discovery learning'. The role of the teacher is to set up tasks that stimulate the student to want to learn about a topic and force them to think deeply about it, for example by testing hypotheses or pursuing alternative lines of enquiry. An appropriate task will stimulate perturbation and so motivate learning. Forcing the learner to think in different ways facilitates the construction of successive mental representations of the topic. Only student-centred tasks that stimulate perturbation and encourage students to employ their reasoning abilities are truly constructivist. Simply setting the task of note taking from a book may have some benefits in the form of varying lesson pace and encouraging students to read their textbook, but without some additional 'twist in the plot' in order to stimulate interest and require the exercise of reasoning, it is not truly in the spirit of constructivist teaching.

Problem-based and enquiry-based learning

Dahlgren and Dahlgren (2002) distinguish between two related approaches to constructivist learning. Problem-based learning (PBL) involves students considering how to use psychological material to solve a tightly defined problem. Enquiry-based learning involves more open tasks, for example preparing debates or presentations on a topic. Both these approaches involve students being presented with a task that involves actively searching for psychological material, selecting from it and applying it to achieve a goal. Both can be carried out individually or collaboratively, using department book stocks, libraries and the Internet. Enquiry-based learning has the advantage of giving the student more freedom to focus on material that stimulates their interest and suits their style of learning (Palmer, 2003). PBL can have the advantage of focusing students on tightly defined topics, important at A-level where there is little time available to diverge from the specification. Boxes 3.1 and 3.2 show examples of enquiry-based and problem-based learning in the psychology classroom.

■ **Box 3.1 Examples of enquiry-based tasks**

■ Prepare a presentation on one theory of forgetting, including its supporting evidence.

■ Produce a poster on the importance of attachment for a child's development.

■ Produce a leaflet on effective stress management that a GP might put in their waiting room.

■ Set out the arguments for the role of either biological factors or psychological factors in one mental disorder.

■ Locate a set of ethical guidelines from the website of the British Psychological Society or the Association for the Teaching of Psychology, and use them to assess the ethics of Milgram's studies of obedience.

■ Using your textbook, find a detailed account of one laboratory experiment. Evaluate it in terms of its ecological validity, replicability and practical applications.

■ **Box 3.2 Examples of problem-based tasks**

■ The victim of a crime has wrongly identified you. Use studies showing that eyewitness testimony in general, and face recognition in particular, can be inaccurate to make your defence.

■ Your local nursery is losing business because of newspaper reports that day care is bad for children's development. Prepare a report challenging this idea that they can show potential parents.

■ A local firm is losing money because their workers are taking so much time off because of work-related stress. Offer them advice on what aspects of people's jobs can cause work-related stress and what strategies they might use to tackle the problem.

■ A character in a television soap opera is being treated unfairly because their behaviour is unusual and eccentric. Your friends ask you as the psychology student to explain the arguments for and against deviation from social norms as a basis for defining someone as abnormal.

■ Social psychology experiments are extremely interesting, but often raise ethical issues. You could not for example replicate the Milgram procedure as a student practical. Design or find an example of a published study in the area of obedience or conformity that would be ethically acceptable.

One of the practical issues we come across in this type of learning is that where students have become used to taking a passive role in the classroom or are highly strategic in their outlook, focusing purely on future grades, they may not take kindly to the shift in responsibility required in problem- and enquiry-based learning. In a recent study of problem-based learning in psychology A-level, Dickson (2010) found that students rated exam-focused lessons as more useful than PBL lessons matched for topic. However, the author points out that this does not mean that PBL is less useful than exam-drilling, rather that students saw it as incongruous with their usual teaching and did not see the benefits. Lee (2004) advocates spending time explaining the procedures and benefits of constructivist tasks of this type before students embark.

Multiple-perspective tasks

Cook (2005) suggests that a further way to force students to actively construct advanced mental representations of a topic is to approach the topic from multiple perspectives. Psychology lends itself to this approach because, for almost any phenomenon or scenario, we can use alternative theories or wider theoretical perspectives to explain what is happening and why. Box 3.3 shows an example of how several social-psychological theories can be used to explain the Holocaust. Box 3.4 shows an example of how alternative psychological perspectives can be used to explain an everyday clinical problem. Note that in both these examples there are multiple cues to guide students towards particular theories and theoretical approaches. Note as well that information has to be not merely retrieved but applied in order to complete the task.

■ **Box 3.3 Multiple-perspective task 1: an example of using theories**

Genocide involves the deliberate and systematic attempt to wipe out a group of people. The best-known historical example of genocide is the Holocaust. In the 1940s in Nazi Germany, under the leadership of Adolf Hitler, more than 6,000,000 people, including Jews, Romanies, trade unionists and people with physical and mental disabilities, were rounded up, sent to concentration camps and murdered. Ordinary people knowingly participated in this process. Hitler was reportedly a highly persuasive speaker, who spent considerable time in speeches emphasising the group identity of the Aryan race and the inferiority of out-groups. The Nazi regime was characterised by the use of visible symbols of authority and the encouragement of highly formal status-based styles of interaction.

Suggest how each of the following theories might provide a partial explanation for the Holocaust.

1 Social identity theory
2 Authoritarian personality theory
3 Agency theory
4 Charismatic leadership

■ **Box 3.4 Multiple-perspective task 2: an example of using psychological approaches** (Adapted from Wilkinson and Campbell, 1997)

John works in an office. He is rather shy and does not feel confident to socialise with his colleagues. Sometimes people take advantage, for example giving him extra work to do, and he tends not to deal with them effectively. One day six colleagues are talking about him and suggest different explanations for his behaviour.

A   It's probably because he had an unhappy childhood. His dad died when he was a child and his mum is really odd.
B   He's just never learned how to act around other people. He never had a male role model and his mum punished him whenever he tried to stick up for himself.
C   He always looks on the downside of everything. He doesn't notice when people are nice to him and he said once that he couldn't remember the last time he had a friend.
D   He's never had the space to grow or be himself. He'd flourish in the right environment.
E   He was probably born like that. People have a certain type of brain and that's that.
F   It's not fair to just look at him as an individual. This office is always really bitchy, and there's a culture here of putting down anyone a bit different.

[a]   Match each of these explanations for John's behaviour to the following theoretical approaches to clinical/abnormal psychology: humanistic, behavioural, psychodynamic, social, biomedical, cognitive.
[b]   Suggest how a psychologist might use each of these approaches to help John.

MAKING LEARNING INTERACTIVE: THE SOCIAL CONSTRUCTIVIST POSITION

The social constructivist position derives from the work of Lev Vygotsky (see Jarvis, 2005 for a review). Note that this approach is very much compatible with the constructivist position – there is simply an additional emphasis on the role of social interaction during learning. Enquiry-based, problem-based and multiple-perspective tasks can be carried out on an individual or co-operative basis. Vygotsky conceived of learning as taking place between a learner and a more advanced peer or adult instructor. He conceived of knowledge as existing initially on an inter-mental plane (i.e. between two people) and only then on an intramental plane (i.e. in the mind of the individual). The difference between what a student can understand working alone and what she can potentially understand through interaction with others is called the zone of proximal development (ZPD). The teacher or advanced peer guides the learner through the ZPD in a process called scaffolding. From the social constructivist perspective the key to effective learning activity is the establishment of purposeful on-task interactions in which one-way or two-way scaffolding can take place. Strategies to establish this type of interaction include collaborative learning and peer tutoring.

Collaborative learning

This can take the form of pair or small group work. The types of task suitable for collaborative learning are not necessarily much different from those that lend themselves to individual active learning. However, there are additional variables to consider because of the group format. Meyers (1997) suggests three aspects of collaborative learning to be considered:

■ *Task structure*: the nature of the task should be amenable to group work, i.e. it must either divide up so that each student can take responsibility for one aspect, or include problems that students can solve through discussion. For example, multiple-perspective tasks work well for groups because each group member can take responsibility for one perspective. For tasks where division of labour is less obvious more substantial teacher input is helpful.

■ *Student assessment*: if marks are to be recorded for the group task we need to be clear in advance how they are to be allocated. Individualised identification of performance may reduce social loafing, however a collective mark may encourage group cohesion.

■ *Group structure*: various strategies can be used to encourage a group to work well together. Drawing on social identity research, Carlsmith and Cooper (2002) suggest that naming groups, encouraging them to sit together in class and sending them to separate areas to work can all increase group cohesiveness.

The limitations of collaborative learning are well documented and, in spite of its potential advantages in terms of encouraging on-task interaction, many commentators believe that these are outweighed by practical difficulties. One problem is timing. By virtue of the time taken to research information, constructivist tasks generally tend to take longer than didactic teaching and this can be exacerbated in collaborative learning when groups spend time negotiating roles, responsibilities and strategies before commencing on a task. This can be tackled by imposing a structure on a group, i.e. allocating tasks. Social loafing is a further issue, as collaboration gives the opportunity for less motivated individuals to participate less actively than would be the case in individual activity. A meta-analysis by Karau and Williams (1993) suggests that social loafing is least in evidence when the following conditions are met:

- When participants believe that their individual contribution can be identified and assessed.
- When the task is important or meaningful.
- When the group is cohesive.
- When individuals believe their own contribution is significant to the end result.
- When the group is small.

The jigsaw technique

A variation on traditional collaborative learning is the jigsaw technique. This makes use of structured worksheets to provide a certain proportion of necessary information, saving research time and focusing student efforts on aspects of the task that require actively using the information. By dividing up elements of the task between group members or whole groups it becomes possible to cover substantial volumes of material in no more time than would have been required for didactic teaching. An example of a lesson using the jigsaw technique to teach media violence is shown in Box 3.5. This lesson can be completed in an hour, certainly no longer than needed for a lecture covering a range of methods used to research the impact of media violence.

Perkins and Saris (2001) have provided evidence for the effectiveness of the jigsaw technique. They divided an undergraduate statistics class into four groups, each completing a different part of an ANOVA test. Student evaluations suggested that the jigsaw technique was an efficient use of class time and enhanced understanding of statistics. A quasi-experimental comparison of student evaluations of the course before and after introducing the jigsaw technique suggested that it significantly enhanced the student experience.

> ■ **Box 3.5 Using the jigsaw technique to teach media violence**
>
> 1 Explanation is provided of social learning theory as a basis for proposing a link between media violence and aggressive behaviour.
> 2 The class is divided into three groups. Each group has a different A3 worksheet outlining one method for researching the effects of media violence – for example, case studies, prospective studies and experimental studies. These provide details of studies and ask questions requiring analytical thinking – for example, in light of research into the characteristics of effective role models, why might fears that the ankle-stabbing scene in *The Evil Dead* could inspire copycat crimes have been unfounded? – and critical thinking – for example, what are the limitations of case studies such as the James Bulger murder as evidence for a link between media violence and aggressive behaviour? The groups jointly answer these questions.
> 3 After a break in which the teacher produces A4 copies of the completed worksheets for all, students individually fill in a pro forma media violence sheet selecting studies and comments from the photocopies.

Peer tutoring

A related strategy involving structured interaction between learners is peer tutoring, in which a more advanced learner takes on the tutor role in order to assist a less experienced or able peer. This replicates the type of interaction that characterises siblings, in which younger children can be observed to develop more rapidly than their older brothers and sisters because of the availability of scaffolding from a more advanced child (Dunn and Munn, 1985). Peer tutoring has been applied to a huge range of age groups, from primary school children to adults in HE.

An example of the use of peer tutoring in post-16 psychology comes from Oley (2002). A total of 65 American students aged 17+ took part. They were set a five-page essay that required considerable background research. In one condition they worked independently. In another peer tutoring was provided. In a third condition peer tutoring from more experienced students was made available as an option. Irrespective of whether the peer tutoring was forced or optional, students benefited from having a peer tutor. Grades were significantly higher and a positive correlation emerged between grade and time spent with peer tutor.

A practical problem to overcome in the use of peer tutors comes in the form of finding the tutors. In the American system in which the Oley study took place tutors were offered course credits. In the UK this is not applicable, however there may be some mileage in writing OCN submissions for short courses in tutoring and marketing these to experienced students, such as those on A2 courses on the basis of gaining teaching experience. Level 3 OCN courses carry UCAS points as well as providing students with useful work experience. See the NOCN website for details of how to write and gain accreditation for this type of course. The web address at the time of writing is www.nocn.org.uk/members/prog-accred.html.

■ **Box 3.6 A checklist for assessing topic delivery for activity and interactivity**

		YES	NO
1	Are there tasks in which students locate information for themselves?		
2	Is there problem-based learning?		
3	Is there enquiry-based learning?		
4	Are there multiple-perspective tasks?		
5	Are students required to think analytically or critically?		
6	Are there tasks that require students to select material for themselves?		
7	Are there collaborative tasks involving division of labour?		
8	Are there collaborative tasks involving joint problem solving?		
9	Are there opportunities for one-to-one coaching of students?		
10	Are there opportunities to provide scaffolding contingent on student progress?		
11	Are there jigsaw tasks?		
12	Is there formal peer tutoring?		
13	Are there opportunities for students to work with peers of different ability?		
14	Is whole-class teaching genuinely interactive?		

MAKING LEARNING RELEVANT: SELECTING AND APPLYING PSYCHOLOGY

It has been a cherished factoid among teachers for many years that 'it doesn't matter what you teach; it's how you do it that counts'. In one sense this is true; what students take away from studying psychology is a set of skills including quite advanced ways of thinking. Years later they will not remember the details of most of the theories and studies you cover in class. However, where there is discretion on a syllabus to choose material, it is still worth considering what topics, theories, studies and examples you will use on the basis that some are inherently more relevant to the lives of students. Recall from Chapter 1 that the most powerful factor affecting students' decision to study psychology is that it is inherently interesting (Hirschler and Banyard, 2003; Walker, 2004). Clearly, the more relevant material is to students the more they will engage with it and the more actively and interactively they will pursue an understanding of it. Relevance can be achieved in several ways.

Topic options

Consider student interest in choosing subject options. For example in the AQA A A2 specification there is choice of applications of psychology from addiction, media or anomalistic psychology. These are all inherently interesting but you and your students might have a view as to which stands out as particularly so. In Edexcel and OCR A2 specs there are a range of applied psychology options, some of which, for example criminological psychology, are often of particular interest to students because they have particular contemporary cultural relevance.

Use of up-to-date material

Consider introducing up-to-date material. There has long been a healthy tension between psychology teachers – at all levels – who emphasise traditional material and those who favour the use of more up-to-date material, in particular studies. Clearly, if we omit seminal studies students miss out on understanding the development of a field. Thus there is a strong case for retaining a degree of traditional material. However, the major advantage of using some more recent studies is that they tend to be more relevant to students. There are, for example, fascinating and accessible contemporary studies of eyewitness memory looking at the 9/11 attacks and studies of helping behaviour that show discrimination against gay people and supporters of rival football teams. These never fail to stimulate lively discussion. Similarly, discursive theory applied to explaining prejudice generally stimulates a debate on the merits of 'politically correct' language. Fitting in this contemporary material necessarily means cautiously looking for traditional material that can be dropped. In Chapter 4 I look at some examples of contemporary studies that lend themselves to practical work as well as enhancing the contemporary relevance of a topic.

Use of news items

Use relevant media stories, in particular those that catch the imagination of students, to bring theory to life. For example, any high profile crime or criminal trial can be used as a stimulus to introduce a multiple-perspective task on explanations for crime. A newspaper article can be used as stimulus material on which questions can be based requiring students to apply theoretical understanding to explain an event or debate. Suggestions for sourcing relevant news stories are made in Chapter 5.

Psychology Applied Learning Scenarios (PALS)

Psychology teaching at all levels has long involved the application of psycholog-ical theory and principles to real-life scenarios. Recently this has been formalised (Norton, 2004) into the notion of PALS. A PALS is a vignette around which will be set one or more tasks designed to stimulate thinking and apply psychological prin-ciples and/or theory. As well as bringing life-relevance to psychological theory, PALS encourage psychological thinking and active learning. Norton's work has been concerned primarily with degree-level psychology, however the technique is applicable to post-16 level. PALS most commonly take the form of problem-based tasks (see p41). Typically the vignette gives details of a current real-life situation and some background information. An example of a PALS is shown in Box 3.7.

■ **Box 3.7 An example of a PALS suitable for post-16 teaching**

Scenario: It is the start of John's first psychology AS exam. This is his first exam and he has never been in the exam hall before. In order to avoid needing the toilet during the exam he has not had his usual coffee that morning. He is feeling tired and rather sluggish. He turns over the paper and sees the first question, which concerns psychodynamic theory. Although the question looks straightforward John finds he cannot recall any of the material.

Background: John has had a traumatic year. His relationship with his parents has deteriorated to the point where he has left home and is staying with friends. He got behind on work earlier in the year and has recently been cramming, revising far into the night and keeping awake by drinking large amounts of coffee.

Tasks

1 Suggest how John's experience of forgetting can be explained in terms of cue dependency. Consider the role of both state and context cues.
2 Suggest a way in which repression might contribute to John's experience of forgetting.
3 Drawing on both theories of forgetting, what might John have done to avoid this experience?

There are a number of factors to consider in the design of vignettes for purposes of PALS (adapted from Norton, 2004).

- The scenario should link easily to recently studied syllabus-relevant theory.
- The scenario should be presented in a real-world context.
- The tasks should have just enough structure to guide students without discouraging independent thinking.
- The scenario and background should contain a number of cues to link into theory. For example, in the above example we are told that John is used to large amounts of coffee – cue for state-dependent forgetting – and that he has not seen the exam hall before – cue for context-dependent forgetting.
- The scenario should be inherently interesting so that thinking is stimulated.

Experiential learning

The term 'experiential learning' has been used very differently in different contexts. Here it is used in a broad sense to refer to any activities in which students have psychology in its research or applied forms conducted on them. This can range from playing the role of participants in professional research to introspective self-analysis.

Research participation

Psychology is a research-based discipline, and a straightforward way for students to experience some 'real' psychology at first hand is for them to take part in academic research as participants. Bowman and Waite (2003) studied the attitudes of American college students to participation in research. Students were offered the choice of writing a short paper or research participation as part of a research methods course. Those who opted to take part in a participant pool to be researched upon rated the research methods course more positively.

So what of the practicalities? Psychology teacher Craig Roberts has pioneered a model of research participation – the 'Psychology Day'. This involves setting aside a day and inviting a range of local universities to submit details of current research projects for which post-16 students might prove suitable participants. The limiting factor that slows the progress of much research is the availability of participants; the opportunity to capture a few dozen participants in a day or half a day is often a heaven-sent opportunity for researchers. There should, therefore, be no shortage of researchers wanting to take part. In return for a steady supply of volunteer participants, researchers are usually more than happy to give detailed debriefs on their studies.

Note that once a range of submissions have been received it is important to vet them for ethical issues. University ethics committees consider the balance of potential benefits and risks of research. Schools and colleges have no such commitment to research, simply a responsibility for the welfare of students. You may, therefore, be rather stricter in drawing the lines about what is acceptable conduct in research. It is also worth involving students at this point to help consider which studies will provide them with an interesting experience. Once studies are approved it just remains to recruit volunteers for the studies.

Introspective tasks

There is a wide range of tasks that require students to introspect and relate psychological material to their own lives. There are, of course, serious ethical issues to consider here; some introspection tasks tread a fine line between teaching and therapy, for which students have not given informed consent and for which most teachers are not qualified. As a general rule steer clear of references to the more intimate and emotionally charged elements of students' own lives, for example parental relationships and mental health problems. It is also worth resisting the temptation to give students personality tests to aid introspection – the humble and omnipresent Eysenck Personality Inventory (EPI) may appear innocuous but in fact contains some very similar items to clinical tests like the Beck Depression Inventory. This can be very upsetting for students who have previously been assessed for depression.

There are, however, ways to use introspection as a teaching tool and stay on safer ground. In introducing social psychological studies that have involved testing both beliefs and behaviour, polls can be conducted; testing for example what proportion of students would obey Milgram's orders and shock Mr Wallace or obey Dr Smith's orders to administer Astrofen were they to find themselves in Hofling *et al.*'s study. In teaching about flashbulb memories it is possible to pick a major event, such as the 9/11 attacks and ask students to recall what they were doing when they heard the news and what peripheral details they can recall. These tasks do require introspection, and by doing so help make psychological research and theory more relevant, but would not normally risk causing distress.

Simulations

It is sometimes possible to simulate the psychological experience being studied. For example, if we are teaching personal space a classic demonstration of the concept is to have students approach a volunteer student until they say 'stop'. At this point you can see their personal space being invaded. Similarly, while you cannot easily replicate the full experience of mental disorder – nor would it be acceptable to do so – you can demonstrate the difficulty experienced by voice-hearers in maintaining auditory attention during a conversation. Have a volunteer – who is aware that they are about to have a slightly unsettling experience – wear headphones and listen to voices from a schizophrenia simulation. There are a number of these available online, for example www.npr.org/programs/atc/features/2002/aug/schizophrenia (requires *RealPlayer*). As the volunteer listens to the voices ask them questions. After a few seconds you will probably find that they need to make an effort to concentrate, and that they start to answer slowly and appear distracted. Be aware of the ethical issues in this kind of simulation. Make sure you have real consent, brief the volunteer fully, check they have no family history of psychosis and don't continue the exercise to a point where they are really struggling.

MAKING LEARNING MEMORABLE: THE ROLE OF INFORMATION-PROCESSING STRATEGIES

Historically there has been a tension between the constructivist ideal in which students learn actively and construct their own individual mental representations of topics, and the information-processing model that emphasises teacher-organisation of material so that it can be made easier to remember. Actually these visions are not irreconcilable; irrespective of what teaching strategies we use to cover specifications students will be assessed by means of exams. This requires that they are helped to organise and learn material, both at the point of delivery and during revision (Gage and Berliner, 1991). Moreover, the depth of processing and elaboration involved in constructivist tasks makes them perfectly compatible with information-processing principles. In fact we can explain the benefits of constructivist tasks in terms of levels of processing (Dickson, 2010).

Tools of organisation: advance and retrospective organisers

Informing students of what is coming at the start of a lesson or topic can be of value in helping them organise the information they then go on to acquire. Ausubel (1968) has called this type of preparation an advance organiser. Advance organisers can take the form of anything that helps students recognise the place of each thing they go on to learn. They can take the form – de rigueur with Ofsted at the time of writing – of putting up aims/objectives of each lesson for students to refer back to as you go. There are however other ways of organising information in advance, for example at the start of a task and at the start of a topic. Three ways of organising material in advance are shown in box 3.8. Note these are just examples and not intended to be definitive.

Note that these sorts of check-lists – especially when structured by topic – are suitable for use as revision check-lists, what we might call retrospective organisers. However, a substantial minority of students benefit significantly from having them at the beginning of topics. A meta-analysis of 135 studies of advance organisation of material (Luiten *et al.*, 1980) showed a small but consistent positive effect to their use, irrespective of age, level and subject. It is likely though that small average effects obscure large effects for particular students – experience suggests that some students benefit enormously from advance organisation.

The role of recall practice: tests and quizzes

One of the most robust effects in the literature of psychology teaching can be found in the benefits of testing students. Testing has a range of potential benefits for students. In cognitive terms it creates recall pathways, facilitating efficient recall under exam conditions. In motivational terms it provides an incentive to keep up with work and to keep material well organised. It thus encourages good study habits.

There are a number of variations in the way we can conduct tests. Leeming (2002) evaluated the 'exam-a-day' approach with four psychology classes at an American college. This involved administering a short test at the start of each lesson then moving on to the normal lesson format. As compared with controls the classes having the 'exam-a-day' had better retention, better student evaluations and better summative test results. The practical limitations of such regular testing include the additional preparation time and the total lost teaching time. The advantages lie in the expertise students gain in recall and the fact that they are well focused on psychology at the start of the normal lesson.

An alternative to every-lesson testing is random administration of tests. An archival study by Sappington *et al.* (2002) showed an association between grades and the use of random quizzes. This is supported by a study by Ruscio (2001), in which college students were administered random quizzes to assess their independent reading. Rates of reading were found to rise significantly.

■ **Box 3.8 Three examples of advance organisation**

1 A lesson

By the end of today's lesson you should be able to:

■ Describe Milgram's classic study of obedience.
■ Outline some variations on the original procedure.
■ Know about ethical issues in research and consider the ethics of Milgram's procedures.
■ Evaluate Milgram's study.

2 A task

The write-up of this practical must be structured into the following sections:

■ Abstract – a short summary of what you did and found.
■ Introduction – a mini-essay on relevant past research.
■ Hypothesis – a prediction of what you expected to find.
■ Method – how you went about the investigation.
■ Results – what you found in the investigation.
■ Discussion – a mini-essay on the implications of your findings.

3 A topic

In clinical psychology you will need to be familiar with the following:

■ two ways of defining abnormality: statistical abnormality + deviation from social norms
■ the DSM system of diagnosis
■ issues of reliability & validity in diagnosis
■ the consequences of receiving a diagnosis
■ cultural issues in diagnosis
■ the biomedical model of abnormality + 1 medical treatment
■ the behavioural model + 1 behavioural therapy
■ the cognitive model + 1 cognitive-behavioural therapy
■ the psychodynamic model + 1 psychodynamic therapy
■ the humanistic model + 1 humanistic therapy
■ the social model + 1 social approach to treatment
■ two mental disorders: symptoms and contributing biological, psychological & social factors

---

Exam prep: the role of metacognitive strategies

At A-level and GCSE preparation for formal assessment primarily involves learning to answer exam questions. Clearly one aspect of this is mastery of the necessary material and practising its recall. However there is a further dimension to exam preparation – learning to interpret and answer questions. Although there are dangers in the strategic model of psychology teaching – constantly emphasising the exam preparation at the expense of fostering enthusiasm and developing transferable skills – we should not assume that students' knowledge and generic skills will necessarily translate into successful exam performance.

So what constitutes effective preparation for exams? Practice certainly, but there is a growing awareness that too much emphasis on simply drilling students with practice questions is ineffective, or at least provides a diminishing return. Moreover, even the most strategic teacher is now in the position of being assessed against *success* rates, i.e. attainment rates of students starting a course rather than those completing it. Once we start to prioritise student retention in order to maximise success rates, then quality of experience becomes more important and it becomes undesirable in every sense to over-assess and demotivate.

A more modern psychological understanding of effective exam preparation may be in terms of students' metacognition. This is a term we often hear nowadays in education, but it has been inconsistently used, leaving many teachers with a vague anxiety that they should but don't understand it! At its simplest, metacognition can be defined as the process of thinking about our own thinking. Larkin has teased this out a little further, providing a helpful definition: 'a form of cognition, a second or higher-level process. It involves both a knowledge of cognitive processing (how am I thinking about this?) and a conscious control and monitoring of that processing (would it be better if I thought about this differently?)' (2002: 65).

The rationale behind much of the current interest in metacognition is that if students have a good metacognitive understanding of what and how they are studying they can better regulate their performance, for example in exams. Flavell (1985) identifies three types of knowledge we make use of in metacognition: personal knowledge, task knowledge and strategy knowledge. These can all be applied to exam preparation.

- *Personal knowledge*: knowledge about ourselves. In relation to exam preparation this might involve students being aware of their vulnerability to exam stress and their personal exam-skill strengths and weaknesses, for example essay-writing, question interpretation and exam timing.
- *Task knowledge*: in terms of preparing students for exams this is particularly important. Students should be aware of the tasks they will face, for example analysing questions and planning answers.
- *Strategy knowledge*: this is related to task knowledge, referring to awareness of how to respond to the tasks they will face.

CONCLUSIONS AND REFLECTIONS

Fashions in teaching can change quickly so it is unwise to identify a 'best' way of teaching psychology. We can, however, abstract from contemporary research a set of principles that can probably be said to reliably enhance learning. The constructivist approach emphasises the role of learning as an active and interactive process. We can make learning psychology an active process by means of enquiry-based,

---

■ **Box 3.9 Metacognitive strategies for exam preparation**

- ■ *Make sure students are fully aware of the assessment objectives and their significance*. This is an essential aspect of task knowledge and a prerequisite for any work done on question analysis.
- ■ *Practice analysing injunctions*. Students frequently lose marks for describing rather than evaluating and – less often – vice versa. One way to tackle this is by exercises, which can be in whole class or small groups in which students explicitly identify the assessment objectives questions are getting at.
- ■ *Practice analysing question content*. Another way in which students lose marks is to misunderstand what content a question requires. One common reason for this is failing to read whole questions in the stress of the exam and responding to the first clause. This can be tackled by group exercises in which students practice breaking down questions.
- ■ *Practice analysing and marking answers*. A useful exercise is for students to practice spotting AO1 and AO2 elements in longer answers. To vary this give some sample answers to AO2 questions where in some cases the answers are AO1 and in others AO2, and have the students identify which answers would score.
- ■ *Experiment with different formats for revision notes*: to develop personal knowledge let students see what format suits their information-processing style. Note that learning style classifications do not have sufficient validity to use as the main basis to advise students about revision notes.

---

problem-based and multiple-perspective tasks. These can be performed individually and collaboratively. Collaboration adds a further dimension to learning, making use of on-task interactions to enhance the quality of student understanding. Jigsaw tasks are a useful way of speeding up collaborative learning, which can otherwise be a slow process. Peer tutoring, while requiring a degree of organisation, can be a highly effective way of providing students with valuable individual scaffolding.

There are, of course, other ways in which learning can be enhanced. Careful selection of psychological material and use of real-life material in the form of media stories and PALS can make psychology more relevant to the experiences of students. Students can also experience some 'real' psychology by participation in professional research – this is easier to organise than we might suspect. Finally, good teaching of a topic can be enhanced from the student perspective by the use of information-processing strategies to make the material more memorable. Advance organisers are one helpful approach. The use of quizzes has been reliably found to improve recall under exam conditions, and metacognitive strategies can further help by ensuring that students do not lose marks by misinterpreting or wrongly answering exam questions.

My approach to this chapter is unquestionably influenced by my view of teaching and learning. I think student experience is important as well as student attainment. I also think learning should be of skills that will benefit students in the long run as well as facts to be regurgitated in an exam then forgotten. These are not universal values, however, and as teachers we all have to decide how important these things are to us personally. I have also based the content of this chapter on theoretical frameworks and evidence where it exists. That's just my way of doing things; some teachers can put together inspiring sequences of learning based purely on creativity and intuition. It is very important that as we move into an era of evidence-based practice we continue to value that kind of artistry.

QUESTIONS FOR REFLECTION

1   How active are students during your lessons?
2   Do you get the balance right between exam-drilling and developing transferable skills?
3   Do your students interact with each other in productive ways?
4   Could you do more to make psychology relevant to the lives of students?
5   Do you use enough strategies to efficiently prepare students for exams?

FURTHER READING

Cook, J.L. (2005) Constructing knowledge: the value of teaching from multiple perspectives. Paper delivered at the NITOP annual conference.

Jarvis, M. (2005) *The psychology of effective learning and teaching*. Cheltenham, Nelson Thornes.

Leeming, F.C. (2002) The exam-a-day procedure improves performance in psychology classes. *Teaching of Psychology* **29**, 210–12.

Norton, L. (2004) *Psychology applied learning scenarios (PALS): a practical introduction to problem-based learning using vignettes for psychology lecturers*. York, LTSN.

CHAPTER 4

PRACTICAL WORK IN THE POST-COURSEWORK ERA

By the end of this chapter you should be able to:

- Take a view on the importance of practical work in contemporary psychology teaching.
- Be aware of some benefits and practical constraints affecting student practical work.
- Implement strategies for the efficient running of student practicals.
- Make ethical decisions about appropriate practical work informed by published ethical principles and guidelines.
- Know examples of successful student practicals, including in areas traditionally regarded as unsuited to practical work.
- Use free on line tools to run student practicals and present and analyse results.

WHY BOTHER?

Psychology is a research-based subject. Perhaps the most important set of transferable skills students take away from studying psychology relate to gathering, analysing and reporting data. This is of use not simply to those going on to study psychology at a higher level but also in a host of employment sectors. More fundamentally, can students really be said to have 'done' psychology if they have not participated in research? When psychology GCSE and A-level had coursework elements the role of practical work was clearly defined. However, since 2008 for A-level and 2009 for GCSE there has been no coursework and, at least for teachers of some specifications, this has led to a lack of clarity about the place of practical work in psychology teaching.

The Qualifications and Curriculum Development Agency (QCDA) rules are clear:

> Due to the potential age of A level candidates and the possible nature of investigative activities in psychology, candidates will not be expected to demonstrate the skills of investigation through internal assessment ... It is expected, however, that candidates should still carry out investigative activities appropriate for the study of psychology at this level. (QC[D]A, 2006: 18)

As teachers have become more strategic, however, the reality has often been that practical work has taken a back seat except in cases where the assessment regime rigorously assesses it. The rigour of this process varies considerably from one awarding body to another.

Benefits of practical work

Idealistically speaking, we should give our students experience of practical work just because it will give them a better experience of studying psychology. Strategically speaking, however, there are some specifications that really require that you do practical work and some that effectively don't. We therefore need to be able to justify in pragmatic as well as idealistic terms why practical work is of benefit for all students. One benefit comes from making research methodology more interesting and relevant and hence more memorable. Remember that intrinsic interest is the main reason students opt for psychology; we need to play that to our advantage.

Taught traditionally, research methods can be immensely dry and quite difficult to relate to real life. If you have a psychology background yourself, think back to your undergraduate statistics lectures – if you haven't repressed them. Probably not your most cherished memories. If you also have research experience, though, you'll know that you actually start to care about the finer points of experimental design and statistical theory when you want to answer your own research questions. Why should this be any different for our students?

We maximise the benefits of practical work when students have an opportunity to give input into design decisions. This is a good opportunity for group work. Students are often more creative than teachers and, given the right guidance and a bit of latitude, will come up with excellent ideas for experiments, observations, correlations and surveys. The role of the teacher in this sort of exercise is to set parameters at the outset – these may be determined by the specification – and to introduce ethical restrictions before practical work is actually carried out.

Time: the limiting factor

The major factor militating against doing practical work – or at least a lot of it – is the time required. There are some tips however to help keep practicals manageable. These all require a bit of preparation, but they do save class time:

■ Some practicals really benefit from student input on the design, for example when teaching research methods. Others are just demonstrations of phenomena that you are studying. The latter don't require much student input; run these in quick time using the students themselves as participants and use the time you save for more demanding practicals.

■ Some practicals, in particular cognitive experiments, can be demonstrated or run online (see p64 for examples). This saves a lot of preparation time, for example in making stimulus materials. For surveys, try putting your questions online, for example with KwikSurveys (www.kwiksurveys.com). You can then have students find respondents and direct them to the site in their own time rather than spending lessons gathering survey data.

■ Focus lesson time on making design decisions and aggregating data. Gathering the data can be a good homework exercise. Some sorts of practical such as content analysis are often easier for students to carry out at home.

■ Sometimes you may want to supervise students as they gather their data, particularly where there may be ethical issues. Where this is the case you will need to use class time to gather data. Brief students explicitly about how many participants they need to find and how long they have to do so.

■ Use online resources to help aggregate data. There are excellent websites that will manage descriptive and inferential statistics for you. This is far quicker than doing it manually. See p66 for a detailed discussion of descriptive and inferential stats packages.

■ Sometimes your anxiety might be not so much about the total lesson time taken to run a student practical as about the risk of time being wasted as some individuals or groups work more efficiently than others. This is a time to employ extension tasks. Suitable extension tasks for practical work include Internet searching for related research, evaluating the methodology and writing up abstracts of the study.

MANAGING ETHICAL ISSUES

We would all agree that ethics are important, even though we might not all draw ethical boundaries in precisely the same place. As the International Union of Psychological Science (2008) put it: 'ethics is at the core of every discipline'. They went on to identify 'a common moral framework that guides and inspires psychologists worldwide toward the highest ethical ideals in their professional and scientific work' (2008: 1). These ethics have been operationalised in a range of codes of principles and guidelines, but it is worth stepping back from these for a moment and reflecting on our shared values and what such codes are meant to achieve.

Psychology has been heavily influenced in its ethical understanding by the philosopher Immanuel Kant, who emphasised the rights of individuals to freedom and self-determination. Kant put it thus: 'Treat humanity in your own person and in others always as an end and never only as the means.' Google put it more succinctly: 'don't be evil'. This understanding of ethics is in marked contrast to the utilitarian approach that dominates management and government. Utilitarianism emphasises the greatest good for the greatest number, with the implication that individual freedom and rights may be compromised for the greater good. If we think of an ethical spectrum between Kantian and utilitarian ideals, psychology is very much at the Kantian end. This brief departure into philosophy is important because it helps us understand why we always have to consider the freedom and dignity of participants as well as their health, and why we have so little wriggle-room in balancing the benefits of research to us or our students against costs to participants.

There are also very sound pragmatic reasons to have high ethical standards. Theodore Kaczynski, better known as the Unabomber, generated the most extensive and expensive manhunt in American history as, between 1978 and 1985, he bombed scientists and universities. Kaczynski had an unremarkable early life until he had a bad experience as a participant in a piece of psychological research, after which he declared a hatred of scientists, including psychologists. Henry Murray was investigating stress responses to aggressive interrogation, and he subjected Kaczynski to 200 hours of verbal aggression and humiliation without informed consent or adequate debrief. We all know the limitations of case study evidence and drawing causal links from possible coincidences, but it is likely that Kaczynski's campaign of terror was a direct result of taking part in what would now be regarded as an unethical study. You wouldn't want to be responsible, even indirectly, for the next Unabomber.

Modern ethical codes

There are several ethical codes we might want to be aware of when conducting practical work. Let's begin with the broadest. The International Union of Psychological Science (IUPS) (2008) identifies four principles guiding ethical codes.

1   *Respect for human dignity*: According to the IUPS respect is the most fundamental principle, and the others follow on from this. This respect applies to individual and cultural diversity, and requires that participants give informed consent free from outside pressure, privacy and confidentiality.

2   *Competent caring*: This means taking care to do no harm in the course of research and taking steps to correct any harm done. It also means working within one's competence. For example, students without specially trained supervisors are not competent to conduct practical work with vulnerable groups such as people with learning disabilities or mental health problems.

3   *Integrity*: This means acting honestly and openly. For example, psychology students at any level should try to minimise bias and avoid exploiting participants for personal gain.

4   *Responsibility to society*: Psychology exists to benefit society, therefore researchers at any level have a responsibility to use their understanding only

for good. Some practicals should be avoided because of their potential for harm, for example reinforcing negative stereotypes of minority or vulnerable groups.

The British Psychological Society (BPS) publishes codes addressing both ethical guidelines and principles. The latest ethical guidelines (BPS, 2009a) are based on the same four principles as defined by the IUPS. It is a document well worth reading in full as it includes practical tips on how to avoid ethical breaches. To pick out and briefly develop a few key points identified in the BPS document:

- Use research evidence where it exists to evaluate a practical for its ethical acceptability. For example at least one study has found that students rated being participants in an Asch conformity replication as distressing. This is a good reason not to run such a study.
- Look where applicable at legal restrictions (see below for more details of relevant legislation).
- Make use of colleagues' advice. In a university environment this is a formal process involving one or more ethics committees. In a school or college there won't be such a body but you can consult colleagues. You can also contact the Association for the Teaching of Psychology or your awarding body for advice.
- Use one or more ethical codes as a check-list to evaluate studies before they are conducted.
- Check with members of the population from which participants will be drawn whether they consider a practical to be ethically acceptable.
- If participants are upset or offended by any procedure your students have run on them, apologise. An apology doesn't diminish your authority or admit legal liability, it simply acknowledges the validity of the offended party's feelings.

Legal issues[1]

You might at first glance think this is overkill on the part of the Nanny State, but there are serious legal issues to be aware of when conducting student practicals. Actually, when you look at the details of legislation it becomes clear that the issues are genuine and sometimes complex. This should not put you off running practicals, just be aware of some pitfalls. One important piece of legislation is the Mental Capacity Act (2005). Under the terms of the MCA it may be an offence to involve a participant in research if they do not have the mental capacity to give real consent (Dobson, 2008). As far as schools and colleges are concerned this means you must avoid research using participants with pervasive learning difficulties or disabilities and participants with mental health problems. Under-16s are not legally deemed competent to give consent either; you will need parental consent to involve them in research.

Article 17 of the Human Rights Act gives the principle of consent legal weight, stating: 'No research on a person may be carried out without the informed, free, express, specific and documented consent of the person' (*Protocol to the Convention on Human Rights in Biomedicine or Biomedical Research*, cited in Velmans *et al.*, 2004: 4). Note the word 'documented'. Effectively this means that you should use consent forms for all student practicals. In the event of a complaint, the onus is on you to prove you took reasonable steps not only to obtain consent, but to document it. Note as well the word 'specific'. The old chestnut of asking consent for a number of studies in which one involves being deceived then just running that one is probably not acceptable under Human Rights law.

Data protection law also becomes important when considering observational research. This is not well known but the 1998 Data Protection Act covers information in video form. Most importantly, you may not film people for research purposes without their knowledge, even if they are in a public place where they may reasonably expect to be observed. Similarly, avoid using web-cams that feed from public places for observations, as you cannot be sure those being filmed have consented.[2] Any film taken for research purposes with participants' consent should not be kept any longer than is necessary for the conduct of the practical. Data protection law also covers the rights of participants not to be identified. This includes in a classroom situation where a class is aggregating the results of a practical. A student who names a participant when contributing individual results into a pool for analysis may be technically in breach of the law.

Ethical principles

The following is summarised from the British Psychological Society's (2009b) *Ethical principles for conducting research with human participants*. You can use this as a check-list to assess student practicals before they are carried out.

1   *Introduction*: There must be mutual respect between researchers and participants for good quality research to take place. This applies to all levels of research including that carried out at school.

2   *General*: All research should be assessed for ethical implications from the viewpoint of participants as well as researchers. The sample population is best placed to judge whether a procedure is acceptable.

3   *Consent*: Where possible, all details of the procedure should be communicated to participants, including any factors that might lead them to refuse to participate. Participants should not be pressured to participate or paid to risk harm. Consent should thus be free and informed.

4   *Deception*: Misleading participants is unacceptable if they are likely to be upset when they discover the deception. All deception should be avoided unless it is essential for the design, and if it is essential it should be disclosed at the earliest opportunity.

5   *Debriefing*: After participating in a study, participants have the right to as

much information as they like about the nature of the study, and to leave the study in at least as positive a mood as they arrived in. If a participant is upset by a procedure they should be told where to seek help – that'd be you.

6 *Withdrawal*: Participants must be told they have the right to withdraw at any point during a study. They also have the right to withdraw their data at the point of debrief.

7 *Confidentiality*: Participants' results and any other information they disclose should be treated as confidential, including when aggregating the results of a class practical.

8 *Protection*: Participants should be protected from harm, including psychological distress. They should not experience any risks over and above those they would normally expect during their daily life.

9 *Observation*: Observers must be sensitive to the privacy and psychological well-being of those being observed, even if they are in a public place.

10 *Advice*: Researchers should not normally give advice to participants, except where to find appropriate help – e.g. school nurse, college counsellor.

11 *Colleagues*: Researchers should advise each other when there is an ethical breach. You as teacher should monitor ethics in all student practicals and act accordingly when there is a breach.

STUDENT PRACTICALS ACROSS THE CURRICULUM: A STUDY FOR ALL SEASONS?

Cognitive psychology

Some topics lend themselves particularly well to practical work while in others it is less obvious. Cognitive topics such as perception and memory are particularly well served by experiments. These raise relatively few ethical issues and can often be run online, making them particularly convenient. Some examples of online cognitive experiments are shown in Table 4.1.

Anomalistic psychology

Similarly well-served is the field of anomalistic psychology. Table 4.2 shows some examples of resources to carry out online parapsychology experiments. The random number generator lends itself to psychokinesis experiments as participants can try to influence the next number to be higher or lower.

Social psychology

Social psychology is a tricky area because, although there are a number of classic social experiments that students would enjoy replicating, many of these raise quite serious ethical issues. Asch and Milgram replications, for example, are not generally considered ethically acceptable nowadays. In fact, experiments in

■ **Table 4.1** Some cognitive practicals and online support

Experiment	Web address
Chunking and capacity of short-term memory	http://www.youramazingbrain.org/yourmemory/chunk01.htm
Serial position curve	http://psych.hanover.edu/JavaTest/CLE/Cognition/Cognition/SerialPosition.html
Memory cues and recall	http://www.youramazingbrain.org/yourmemory/capital_cities.htm
Smells as memory cues	http://www.bbc.co.uk/science/humanbody/mind/surveys/sniffingthedecades/
Accuracy of witness memory	http://www.youramazingbrain.org/testyourself/eyewitness.htm
Stroop test with variations	http://faculty.washington.edu/chudler/words.html
Extroversion and mental rotation	http://www.bbc.co.uk/science/humanbody/mind/surveys/neckercube/
Reaction time	http://faculty.washington.edu/chudler/java/reacttime.html
Poggendorf illusion	http://psych.hanover.edu/JavaTest/CLE/Cognition/Cognition/poggendorf_instructions.html
Various illusions	http://dragon.uml.edu/psych/illusion.html

■ **Table 4.2** Anomalistic psychology online experiments

Random number generator	http://www.random.org/integers/
Psychokinesis testers	http://www.fourmilab.ch/rpkp/experiments/
Precognition tester	http://www.pni.org/esp/dice/
Unseen staring detecter	http://www.psychicscience.org/staring.aspx
Clairvoyance detector	http://www.psychicscience.org/esp3.aspx

social psychology are generally worth steering clear of. However, with a bit of lateral thinking it is quite possible to think of non-experimental social practicals to partially replicate. These are just a few examples.

■ Crandall *et al.* (2002): normative influence on prejudice. This can be used as a practical when studying either conformity or prejudice. The aim is to look at the correlation between personal and normative prejudices. Identify a range of groups, taking care to avoid any that will be too sensitive given the demographics of your students. You are usually on safe ground with predatory paedophiles as a group high in normative prejudice and cat-owners representing low prejudice – see the original paper for the full range. Participants rate each group on the basis of how acceptable or unacceptable it is to be prejudiced against them. They also rate how personally prejudiced they are towards each group. Aggregate the data so there is an average personal prejudice score and a normative prejudice score for each group. Plot these on a scatterplot so that each point represents one target group. Crandall and colleagues found a correlation of +0.96 between personal and normative prejudice, one of the strongest relationships anywhere in psychology.

■ Geher *et al.* (2002): estimates of self and other obedience rates in the Milgram experiment. This makes a good introductory activity for the study of Milgram. The aim of the study is to see how accurate people are in their estimates of the maximum voltage people would administer in the Milgram situation. An additional twist to the study is in looking for a difference between estimates of what voltage people thought they would give themselves and what voltage they thought a typical other would give. Geher and colleagues found that participants estimated 139V for themselves and 210V for others. The actual mean average Milgram found was 368V. The study illustrates how poor we are at judging the extent of human obedience, particularly in relation to ourselves.

■ Blass and Schmitt (2001): attribution of responsibility in the Milgram experiment. This is a useful study for looking at why participants might have been so obedient in the Milgram experiment. Students watch video footage of the Milgram procedure and attribute responsibility to the experimenter and to the participant. Blass and Schmitt found that participants overwhelmingly blamed the experimenter rather than the participant. This illustrates one of Milgram's initial explanations for his findings – that participants did not feel responsible for their actions. It is also consistent with his later agency theory.

Developmental psychology

Some areas of the curriculum are tricky to pepper with practicals. Developmental psychology at GCSE and A-level overwhelmingly focuses on young children. It was once the norm to conduct observations and experiments in nurseries or primary schools, but a combination of tighter ethical boundaries, modern safeguarding procedures, time constraints and strategic thinking means this practice has all but disappeared. Piaget tasks can be replicated with 16+ participants (if you've never seen A-level students play with Playdoh in their investigation of mass conservation it's worth a look!) but without access to children of the ages Piaget was studying it is questionable how useful this is. And what about attachment? This is the first area of developmental psychology encountered by most students and it is inherently sensitive – you don't want students going around classifying babies as insecurely attached willy nilly.

Adult attachment is no less sensitive. Enter Harry Potter – or other famous and lovable fictional characters. One of the most interesting aspects of modern attachment research is parasocial attachment – attachment to fictional characters. Cohen (2004) classified participants as types A, B or C attachment by having them choose between three paragraphs describing their relationships. They were then asked to think of their favourite fictional character and imagine their loss, then fill in a questionnaire. Type Cs reported that they would experience more distress if their character died than did types A and B. We are on dodgy ethical ground if we, or our students, classify people by attachment type, but they can be classified by parasocial attachment type. It is straightforward to alter the wording of an attachment classification system to refer to participants' perceptions of their relationship to fictional characters rather than real people.

Abnormal psychology

Abnormal psychology similarly requires a bit of lateral thinking, given that we cannot study people suffering from mental health problems. Surveys looking at social stigmatisation of mental health may be possible but require some safeguards, such as ensuring that those currently dealing with mental health issues are not left struggling with the additional issue of learning the extent of prejudice against their condition. Content analysis comes into its own here; past studies have shown that media coverage of mental health tends to be very negative (see for example the work of Greg Philo). If you are studying eating disorders a useful practical can involve content-analysing magazines for numbers of small, average and larger models illustrated in adverts and/or articles.

These are just a few illustrative examples of practical work. You may have other ideas that work better for you. The point is that it is possible to get some sort of practical work into most areas of the curriculum if you wish.

USING TECHNOLOGY TO PRESENT AND ANALYSE RESULTS

One of the major time constraints that limits practical work is the time required to do anything meaningful with the raw data. This is a case for the appliance of some technology.

Presenting results in graphical form

There are a number of free programs and Internet sites that will allow you to produce graphs of your results. For converting raw data quickly into graphs I particularly like the set of tools from Utah State University: http://nlvm.usu.edu/en/nav/topic_t_5.html. Here you can very quickly produce box plots, bar charts, pie charts and scatter-plots. The latter tool is particularly helpful because you can plot directly on to the graph as well as into a spreadsheet, and the coefficient appears and changes instantly with each new data point (see Figure 4.1).

Inferential statistics

Software that performs statistical analysis has been around in various forms since the 1960s. Early programs tended to be unwieldy and required considerable knowledge of programming. Although many statistics aficionados still opt for this type of program, there are now a number of packages available with extremely

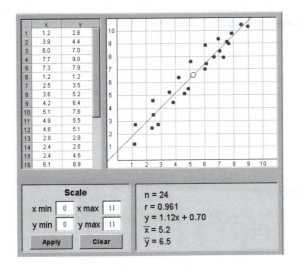

	x	y
1	1.2	2.8
2	3.9	4.4
3	6.0	7.0
4	7.7	9.0
5	7.3	7.9
6	1.2	1.2
7	2.5	3.5
8	3.6	5.2
9	4.2	6.4
10	5.1	7.6
11	4.9	5.5
12	4.6	5.1
13	2.8	2.8
14	2.4	2.5
15	2.4	4.6
16	6.1	8.9

Scale

x min 0 x max 11
y min 0 y max 11

Apply   Clear

n = 24
r = 0.961
y = 1.12x + 0.70
$\bar{x}$ = 5.2
$\bar{y}$ = 6.5

■ **Figure 4.1** Utah State University's correlation plotting tool (http://nlvm.usu.edu/en/nav/topic_t_5.html)

user-friendly spreadsheet-type graphical user interfaces (GUIs). These perform a range of descriptive and inferential statistics. In the 1990s a low-cost and fairly user-friendly inferential stats package called stATPack was developed and sold by the Association for the Teaching of Psychology (Haworth, 1997). When stATPack was withdrawn after it emerged that some critical values were incorrect, the attention of psychology teachers shifted away from statistical software and has largely stayed away since.

Much has changed, however, since the withdrawal of stATPack. Most importantly, the Internet has developed out of all recognition and with it has grown a movement for the distribution of free and open source software (FOSS). In this climate it is quite straightforward to obtain statistical analysis software free of charge. Of course a lot depends on what we mean by 'free' (Grant, 2004). Although the software reviewed in this study is all free in monetary terms at the point of delivery, for a teacher exploring without help there can be considerable indirect costs in terms of the time required to track down, install and evaluate a range of packages.

One reason why little has been written about free statistical software in the psychology teaching literature is that universities and commercial research organisations generally have subscriptions to commercial packages; hence staff can access very powerful and comprehensive software with comparative ease. The situation is obviously different in schools and colleges where budgets are far smaller. At the time of writing the UK 'industry standard' statistical package, SPSS, charges around £1,000 a year for a site licence for their basic package, way out of reach for schools. There are additional problems with using SPSS for teaching purposes. The tables of results generated for each analysis are unnecessarily complex (MacCrae, 2005 personal communication). We – let alone students! – can easily be left having to sift through this for the information we want and feeling rather inadequate at how much of the information we don't understand. Another problem is that SPSS cannot be run on a network and must therefore be loaded separately on to each machine, from where it cannot be remotely accessed. While most of the free software reviewed here is ultimately less powerful and versatile than SPSS, much of it is probably better suited to introductory level teaching simply because it is so much simpler and more comprehensible. Twelve systems are assessed here against the following criteria:

■ Coverage of the inferential tests usually taught at post-16 level.
■ Good range of additional tests for purposes of demonstration or teacher research.
■ Resemblance to SPSS – i.e. good preparation for psychology at HE level.
■ Ability to work with Excel files.
■ Ability to run on a network.

Table 4.3 shows the coverage of the basic inferential tests commonly taught at post-16 level.

Most packages were found to run Chi^2 and t-tests. Only Pearson's product moment was found in all programs – although in the cases of SSP and Statuccino this had to be extracted from the regression function. Four packages were found to be complete in running all the inferential tests commonly taught at post-16 level. These were Merlin, OpenStat, SalStat and BrightStat. Table 4.4 shows how well each package fared against additional criteria.

■ **Table 4.3** Coverage of inferential tests in free software

Package	Chi^2	Sign test	Pearson's	Spearman's	t-test	Mann-Whitney	Wilcoxon
Downloads							
Merlin	√	√	√	√	√	√	√
OpenStat	√	√	√	√	√	√	√
Statlets	√		√	√	√		√
PAST	√		√	√	√	√	
SSP	√		√		√		
Instat+	√		√		√		
Statuccino			√		√		
Qmulate	√		√		√		
SalStat	√	√	√	√	√	√	√
AM			√				
Online							
VassarStat	√		√	√	√	√	√
BrightStat	√	√	√	√	√	√	√

■ **Table 4.4** Evaluation of free statistical software against other post-16 psychology criteria

Package	Range of additional tests	Preparation for SPSS use in HE	Works with Excel files	Can be run on a network
Downloads				
Merlin	√		Imports & exports as Excel files	√
OpenStat	√√	√√	Imports & exports text files	√
Statlets	√	√	Imports & exports text files	Not free version
PAST	√√	√	Imports & exports text files	√
SSP	√			
Instat+	√	√	Imports & exports as Excel files	√
Statuccino	√			√
Qmulate			Requires DOS commands	√
SalStat	√√	√	Imports & exports text files	√
AM	√	√	Imports & exports as Excel files	√
Online				
VassarStat	√		Cut and paste from Excel	N/A
BrightStat	√	√	Imports & exports Excel files	N/A

Three packages satisfied all the criteria against which I evaluated them. These were OpenStat, SalStat and BrightStat. Merlin, VassarStat and PAST also emerged as extremely useful. All of these are thus recommended. Current URLs are shown in Box 4.1.[3]

OpenStat was developed by retired professor of psychology Bill Miller. It was designed with psychology in mind and carries out an enormous range of statistical tests. Its interface is virtually identical to that of SPSS, both in capabilities and layout. This makes it the best package for preparation for statistics at HE level. SalStat was developed by Cardiff University human–computer interaction expert Alan Salmoni. The interface is similar to OpenStat and SPSS in that it has a drop-down menu over a spreadsheet. Unlike OpenStat, SalStat can import and export

---

■ **Box 4.1 Current URLs for recommended inferential stats software**

OpenStat http://www.statpages.org/miller/openstat/
Brightstat http://www.brightstat.com
SalStat http://directory.fsf.org/math/stats/SalStat.html
VassarStat http://faculty.vassar.edu/lowry/VassarStats.html
PAST http://folk.uio.no/ohammer/past/
Merlin http://www.heckgrammar.kirklees.sch.uk/

to Excel without the hassle of converting to text files – a very useful time-saving feature. However, at the time of writing SalStat is only available time-limited – you have to download it again every few months. BrightStat differs from OpenStat and SalStat in that it runs from an Internet site rather than as a downloadable programme. Users need to register individually before they can access tests, but this is free and registered users can store files on the website. Merlin was developed by Neil Millar for Heckmondwike Grammar School, Kirklees. Although it was developed with biology A-level in mind it includes all the tests needed for post-16 psychology. Merlin differs from the other programs reviewed here in that it is an Excel add-in. If you like Excel – I don't – this may be the package of choice for you.

CONCLUSIONS AND REFLECTIONS

We return here to the balance between strategic and holistic teaching. Strategically speaking you may have to do lots of practical work or little or none according to your choice of specification. To me though this is missing the point. Practical work, if well managed, is a positive experience for everyone involved and helps develop transferable skills and student enthusiasm. It may also make material more memorable and so aid exam performance. There are practical, ethical and even legal limitations to what practical work can be carried out and how it needs to be managed, but these issues can be dealt with and should not put you off. In particular, spend some time thinking outside the box about what practicals to run, and experiment with the use of time-saving technology. In particular, take the time to master a free inferential stats package. Think as well about what practicals can be run as quick demos and which would really benefit from more substantial student input.

QUESTIONS FOR REFLECTION

1   Do you do practical work with your students? If not what might the benefits be?
2   How can you manage practical work quickly and efficiently?
3   In what ways can you manage ethical issues in student practicals?
4   How imaginative are you in thinking up practical activities?
5   How might technology be used to enhance student practicals?

NOTES

1   This advice is given in good faith but is intended as a general guide only. I am no lawyer. If in doubt about any of these issues it is important to consult a member of the legal profession. Your employer or trade union may be able to help with this.
2   Animal rights legislation is different in focus. You can use zoo-cams to observe animal behaviour (see Chapter 7 for a discussion).
3   These URLs are correct at the time of writing. They may change however. To keep up to date try freestatistics.altervista.org/stat.php

FURTHER READING

BPS (2009) *Ethical principles for conducting research with human participants*. Leicester, British Psychological Society.

BPS Ethics Committee (2009) *Code of ethics and conduct*. Leicester, British Psychological Society.

International Union of Psychological Science (2008) *Universal declaration of ethical principles for psychologists*. Berlin, IUPS

CHAPTER 5

TEACHING PSYCHOLOGICAL THINKING

By the end of this chapter you should be able to:

- Be clear about the importance of developing psychological thinking in students.
- Describe Bloom's taxonomy of thinking skills and understand its application in assessing A-levels.
- Consider the relationship between psychological thinking and scientific thinking and discuss the dual role of analytic and synthetic thinking in psychology.
- Apply an understanding of higher-level psychological thinking to assessing student work, with particular regard to the work of Peter Facione.
- Understand how to use a range of activities to develop higher-level thinking in the psychology classroom, including the use of elaborated evaluation, repertory grids and evaluation toolkits.
- Outline, apply and evaluate Sternberg's triarchic model of psychology teaching.

Psychology is as much a way of thinking as it is a collection of knowledge, theory and research. What distinguishes a good psychologist or psychology student? It is probably not just how much they know but how deeply and effectively they can think about the subject. As B.F. Skinner reportedly remarked, education is 'what is left when you've forgotten what you've learnt' (cited in Swansea University student bar). Much of what the successful psychology student takes away from the subject is in the form of thinking skills. So far, so good, but exactly what sort of thinking are we talking about? How are thinking skills tied into the psychology curriculum and what strategies can psychology teachers use to assess and develop them? The aim of this chapter is to answer these rather lofty questions in terms of practical classroom solutions.

WHAT ARE THINKING SKILLS AND WHY DO THEY MATTER?

Advantages conferred by advanced thinking

In education generally there has been a significant shift over the past decade towards making the development of thinking skills a priority. This is reflected in both the use of sophisticated assessment objectives in contemporary GCSE and A-level curricula, and in the adoption of personal, learning and thinking skills (see for example http://curriculum.qcda.gov.uk/uploads/Personal,%20learning%20 and%20thinking%20skills%20leaflet_tcm8-12831.pdf). This is widely believed to be important for both the individual and society. On the societal level thinking skills are likely to become increasingly important in tackling world problems. Philosopher Richard Paul refers to the 'deep-seated problems of environmental damage, human relations, overpopulation, rising expectations, diminishing resources, global competition, personal goals and ideological conflict' (1993: 1) that face future generations and will require imaginative and critical thought to tackle.

On the level of the individual, Wilson (2000) suggests that a broad range of higher thinking skills is beneficial on the grounds of cognitive efficiency. In the current climate, in which the volume of information we are required to process is ever increasing, we simply cannot store sufficient information to respond to every situation without being able to transfer skills from one situation to another. This can be very important at A-level. Consider the long-term memory load for an A-level student preparing for an exam in which they can be asked to evaluate one or more of dozens of empirical studies. To learn a toolkit of evaluation skills involves higher-level thinking and so is initially a difficult task. However, once achieved, the student can go into the exam without having had to rote-learn separate evaluation points for a large number of studies. In terms of cognitive load this is a much more efficient strategy.

There are also more distal advantages to enhancing students' thinking skills. Higher-level thinking skills are important when we come to consider preparing students for study at higher education (HE) level. There is research to show that students with good higher-level thinking skills do better in psychology degrees. In an American study, Williams *et al*. (2003) assessed 149 psychology undergraduates for thinking skills and found that critical thinking as assessed at the start of the course correlated (r=0.41) with exam performance, accounting for 26% of the variance in results. Although thinking skills were found to improve during the course this still shows that the starting point for thinking skills at entry to HE is significant.

In a fascinating account of a workshop for HE teachers on post-16 psychology run as part of the Writing in the Disciplines project (see www.learndev.qmul.ac.uk for details), Tombs (2004) reported that HE teachers tended to be surprised and impressed by the volume of information covered at A-level, but critical of the superficial evaluation skills usually developed and of the lack of time allowed by the specifications for students to develop a sophisticated mental representation of psychological material. This is an extremely important point; as the awarding bodies face allegations of 'dumbing down' it becomes increasingly difficult politically for curriculum developers to produce a less content-laden syllabus that better lends itself to the development of advanced thinking skills. It thus falls to the psychology teacher to use effective strategies to promote higher-level thinking.

Bloom's taxonomy and psychology

The term 'thinking skills' is not a clear one, and some commentators have questioned whether we are technically correct to think of cognitive processes as skills that can be learned in the same way as motor skills (Wilson, 2000). Helpfully, Wilson has redefined the central question facing teachers and researchers as 'can [students] be taught to think more effectively?' (2000: 2). When we speak of 'thinking' in this context we are not referring so much to the stream of consciousness that describes our moment-by-moment experience of thinking, but rather a set of higher order mental processes. There have been a number of attempts to classify such higher-order processes. Particularly influential at A-level has been the taxonomy developed by Bloom (1956). This is shown in Figure 5.1.

To Bloom and colleagues there were six levels of thinking, which we can think of as the cognitive goals of education. These were seen as an ascending hierarchy, the most basic being knowledge and the highest evaluation. Bloom's approach has been enormously influential in curriculum design and assessment. Consider the assessment objectives adopted by the awarding bodies for post-2000

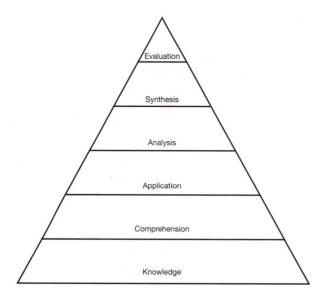

■ **Figure 5.1** Bloom's taxonomy

A- and AS-levels. These are framed in terms of assessment objectives, one representing Bloom's basic levels of knowledge and understanding and another representing their higher goals. In keeping with the belief that analysis, synthesis and evaluation represent more advanced levels of thinking, the proportion of marks available for AO2 is greater at A2 than AS level.

- *Knowledge*: Knowledge of a subject is shown by identifying, defining and outlining psychological ideas, theories, studies and applications. This is the simplest form of thinking to teach and assess, and does not require higher-level thinking.
- *Understanding*: Understanding is demonstrated by rephrasing, clarifying, explaining and drawing conclusions from psychological material.
- *Application*: Application takes place when an understanding of theory and/or research is used to explain a scenario such as a real-life situation.
- *Analysis*: Analysis involves going beyond the obvious information, breaking down a concept or situation in order to better understand it. This might, for example, involve suggesting where an idea came from or what factors might underlie a situation.
- *Synthesis*: This is roughly equivalent to the concept of creativity. Synthesis takes place when we put ideas together in an imaginative way, perhaps designing a new programme or improving an existing theory or research method.
- *Evaluation*: This is roughly equivalent to the concept of critical thinking. Evaluation is demonstrated when we make judgements about an idea, theory, study or practice. How to evaluate theories and studies is addressed in detail on p82.

Fisher (1995, adapted for A-level by Jarvis, 2005) has offered a set of injunctions designed to cue students to employ each of Bloom's thinking skills. These may be of use in both class discussions and written tasks. These are shown in Table 5.1.

■ **Table 5.1** Question injunctions as thinking process cues

Level	Thinking skill	Cues for classroom exercises
1	Knowledge	Describe, outline, recall, repeat, define, identify, which, where, who, what?
2	Understanding	Summarise, rephrase, explain, conclude, relate, interpret, why?
3	Application	Demonstrate, apply, use to solve, use to explain.
4	Analysis	Identify the causes, compare, reasons, problems, solutions, consequences.
5	Synthesis	Develop, improve, design, create, put together, tell a story.
6	Evaluation	Judge, criticise, evaluate the success, practical value, coherence, validity.

Psychological thinking and scientific thinking

In its early days, psychology struggled for recognition as a science, and some of the early movements in psychology, most obviously behaviourism, based their credibility on their visible scientific credentials. The situation has changed and the question is no longer so much 'is psychology a science?' but rather 'given psychology's diversity and that it is classified as a science, what is science itself?' A full discussion of the relationship between psychology and science is not within the scope of this book, but it has clear implications for defining what we mean by psychological thinking. In other words, is psychological thinking the same as scientific thinking? According to McGhee (2001) the answer is a resounding 'no'. A good psychologist must be able to think like a scientist but also, on occasion, like an anthropologist, a historian, a philosopher and a therapist. This is a challenging idea for psychology teachers at both school and undergraduate level who (necessarily) spend considerable time inculcating in students an understanding of the scientific method. However, although we place considerable value on psychology as a science, even at introductory levels we do teach and value other ways of thinking, albeit often implicitly.

Time to get more technical. One way to understand the range of thinking that we might call 'psychological' is with reference to the distinction between analytic and synthetic modes of thinking (Sternberg, 1997; McGhee 2001). In this context, the terms analysis and synthesis are used more broadly than in Bloom's model. Analytic thinking is logical, based on drawing inferences from available data. Synthetic thinking, on the other hand, is free flowing and imaginative. We think analytically when we apply rules to decide the truth or falsity of an explanation, when we statistically analyse data and when we design an experiment to eliminate the influence of all independent variables bar the one we are interested in. This is very much traditional scientific thinking and many psychologists think of it as the correct way to think about psychology.

Without a degree of synthetic thinking, however, sciences never make great leaps. As McGhee puts it: 'It is the imaginative leaps carried out by Copernicus, Albert Einstein and Stephen Hawking that set them apart from their merely excellent peers' (2001). Whenever we generate a new hypothesis to test a theory, use an analogy to make a model accessible – such as the multistore model – or apply a psychological theory or idea to understanding a new situation, we are thinking synthetically. But what does this scientific philosophy have to do with classroom teaching? The answer is that being able to appreciate both analytic and synthetic thinking allows students to think more widely when looking for the commentary and evaluation that comprise AO2 marks. This is put into practice in designing thinking skills toolkits (see p82) and is reflected in the type of sequenced learning activities that follow from Sternberg's triarchic model of psychology teaching (p86).

Analysing thinking skills

It can be instructive to teachers and students to be aware of the extent to which students are using higher-level thinking. Advanced thinking skills can be assessed by means of psychometric tests, such as the California Critical Thinking Dispositions Inventory (CCTDI), shown in Box 5.1. Note that the term 'critical thinking' is used here in a broad sense to mean higher-level thinking. In other contexts it is used more narrowly to mean evaluation.

However, most psychology teachers are not qualified to administer psycho-metric tests for diagnostic purposes – using them for demonstration and research purposes are greyer areas. This requires the British Psychological Society's Statement and Certificate of Competence in Educational Testing. Moreover, if anything students are already over-assessed and at risk of labelling effects. An alternative is to assess existing written work. The simplest way of doing this is by means of published mark schemes from the awarding bodies. However. these tend to give at least limited credit to brief or formulaic evaluation and analysis (Tombs, 2004). This means that students can learn to survive the exam system without developing the thinking skills that would gain them the top marks and be transfer-able to other contexts. A way around this is to use Facione and Facione's (1994) Holistic Critical Thinking Scoring Rubric. This is shown in Box 5.2.

Because it is not tied to any particular mark scheme, Facione's rubric may provide a better general tool for assessing the sophistication of thinking in students' written work. It can be used to show students directly what they are doing correctly and incorrectly. This is often not easy by means of published mark schemes. Remember that these are constructed primarily to achieve acceptable levels of reliability and validity in the marking process, not to give students forma-tive feedback. For more information about Facione's rubric see http://www.insigh-tassessment.com/pdf_files/rubric.pdf.

■ **Box 5.1 The California Critical Thinking Dispositions Inventory** (Facione, 1995)

This has 75 items, measuring seven subscales of critical thinking: truth seeking, open-mindedness, analyticity, systematicity, self-confidence, inquisitiveness and maturity. Answers are by means of a six-point Likert scale (strongly agree – strongly disagree).

Examples of items include the following;

☐ Studying new things all my life would be wonderful   (assesses inquisitiveness)

☐ It is impossible to know what standards to apply to most questions   (assesses analyticity)

☐ I believe what I want to believe   (assesses open-mindedness)

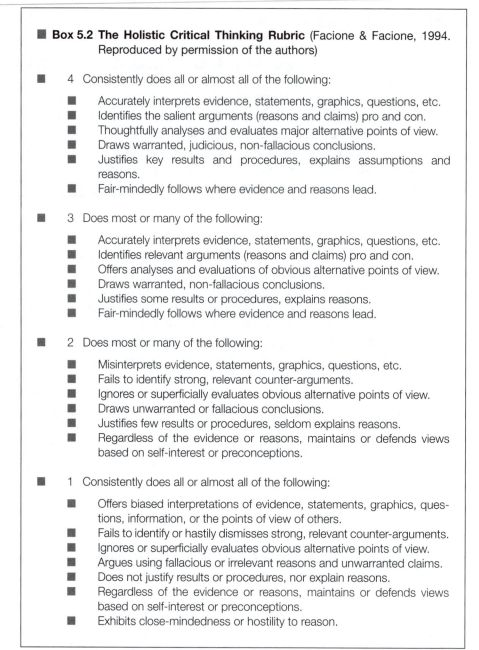

■ **Box 5.2 The Holistic Critical Thinking Rubric** (Facione & Facione, 1994. Reproduced by permission of the authors)

■ 4 Consistently does all or almost all of the following:

- ■ Accurately interprets evidence, statements, graphics, questions, etc.
- ■ Identifies the salient arguments (reasons and claims) pro and con.
- ■ Thoughtfully analyses and evaluates major alternative points of view.
- ■ Draws warranted, judicious, non-fallacious conclusions.
- ■ Justifies key results and procedures, explains assumptions and reasons.
- ■ Fair-mindedly follows where evidence and reasons lead.

■ 3 Does most or many of the following:

- ■ Accurately interprets evidence, statements, graphics, questions, etc.
- ■ Identifies relevant arguments (reasons and claims) pro and con.
- ■ Offers analyses and evaluations of obvious alternative points of view.
- ■ Draws warranted, non-fallacious conclusions.
- ■ Justifies some results or procedures, explains reasons.
- ■ Fair-mindedly follows where evidence and reasons lead.

■ 2 Does most or many of the following:

- ■ Misinterprets evidence, statements, graphics, questions, etc.
- ■ Fails to identify strong, relevant counter-arguments.
- ■ Ignores or superficially evaluates obvious alternative points of view.
- ■ Draws unwarranted or fallacious conclusions.
- ■ Justifies few results or procedures, seldom explains reasons.
- ■ Regardless of the evidence or reasons, maintains or defends views based on self-interest or preconceptions.

■ 1 Consistently does all or almost all of the following:

- ■ Offers biased interpretations of evidence, statements, graphics, questions, information, or the points of view of others.
- ■ Fails to identify or hastily dismisses strong, relevant counter-arguments.
- ■ Ignores or superficially evaluates obvious alternative points of view.
- ■ Argues using fallacious or irrelevant reasons and unwarranted claims.
- ■ Does not justify results or procedures, nor explain reasons.
- ■ Regardless of the evidence or reasons, maintains or defends views based on self-interest or preconceptions.
- ■ Exhibits close-mindedness or hostility to reason.

STRATEGIES TO DEVELOP THINKING SKILLS

All psychology teachers working at all levels constantly use multiple strategies to encourage students to think beyond Bloom's basic levels of knowledge and understanding. Whenever we pose a question to a group, praise a creative response to psychological material or discuss the strengths and weaknesses of a study, theory or method we are promoting higher-level thinking. The strategies discussed in this chapter are in the form of tasks and prompts specifically designed to push students to think in advanced ways to which they might not be accustomed. In an influential report Carol McGuinness (1999) concluded that, irrespective of different theoretical bases, alternative approaches to developing thinking skills share the ultimate goal of bringing about qualitative change in the type of thinking of which learners are capable. In terms of their rationale for doing this they tend to share a number of core concepts:

- Learners are active creators of their knowledge, thus it is necessary for learners to seek meaning and impose structure on learning material as opposed to passively absorb it. Development of thinking skills is thus closely related to the constructivist tradition (discussed in Chapter 3).
- A classroom focus on thinking skills is beneficial because it leads to development of activities that support active information-processing strategies.
- Learners can be and need to be taught the skills of higher-level thinking.
- Development of thinking skills requires a taxonomy of skills to be developed or selected. That of Bloom is an example of a thinking skills taxonomy.
- Effective teaching of thinking skills involves developing non-routine tasks, which require higher-level thinking to complete successfully.
- Learners need to develop better awareness of their own thought processes and to reflect consciously on them. This type of awareness is called metacognition.
- There are important social aspects to learning, and learners pick up thinking strategies from each other and from teachers. Social interaction should thus be oriented towards a thinking skills perspective.
- Thinking takes place in a cultural context, and the culture of the learning environment must reflect the value placed on thinking skills. Thus questioning and challenge should be encouraged.
- Teachers and institutions can benefit from improvements in thinking skills as well as individual learners.

AO2 elaboration exercises

Assessment Objective 2 is meant to assess and so encourage the development of higher-level thinking skills. However, AO2 and higher-level thinking are not synonymous. While it is probably necessary to think deeply about psychological material to gain high AO2 marks, some marks can be gained by brief, superficial and formularised comments. One way to encourage psychological thinking that directly impacts both proximally on AO2 marks and distally on thinking skills is to elaborate AO2 answers. A useful strategy to begin this process can be to deny students the tools for producing formulaic answers. Thus the term 'ecological validity', which is – sometimes indiscriminately – scattered throughout A-level exams without elaboration, may be best not introduced until students have a thorough understanding of the significance of the environment in which studies are conducted.

A three-stage strategy to elaborate AO2 answers

1   The initial exercise is to have students analyse the differences between exam-
     ples of superficial and elaborate evaluation. This both puts their analytical
     skills to work and provides a template for what an elaborated AO2 answer
     looks like. It is heavily cued by the use of specific questions. If we think in
     terms of evaluation being picked up across a zone of proximal development
     these cues provide the scaffolding. An example is shown in Box 5.3.
2   The next stage is for students to take examples of superficial evaluation
     and develop them into an elaborated form. This is a more autonomous task,
     however the stimulus of the superficial evaluation provides a degree of scaf-
     folding. An example is shown in Box 5.4.
3   The third stage is to put the understanding and practice developed in the first
     two stages into practice by administering AO2 questions. The twist in the
     plot at this point is to not give mark allocations with the questions. The task
     is for students to write as much as they can without distraction thoughts about
     whether they have reached the maximum mark.

■ **Box 5.3 An example of analysing the differences between superficial and elaborated evaluation**

Question: Discuss the ethical issues associated with Milgram's obedience experiment.

Answer 1

Milgram was unethical. He lied to participants and told them they couldn't leave. It also lacked ecological validity.

Answer 2

Milgram's work took place before the development of ethical guidelines so it is question-able whether he should be judged retrospectively by these standards. Milgram misled participants about the point of the experiment and that Mr Wallace was badly hurt or dead. This, of course, was necessary for the experiment to work. He also caused them distress and, most seriously, he denied them the right to withdraw. On the other hand he debriefed them and followed them up to make sure they were all right.

Questions

1   Both answers are evaluations of Milgram. Which answer focuses better on the issue of ethics?
2   How does answer 2 set Milgram's work in context?
3   What blunt statements are made in answer 1 make that could be expanded upon?
4   Answer two is more balanced. In what ways does it put across both sides of the argument?
5   Give one mark for each fully made point to each answer. As marker, what would you give each answer?

■ **Box 5.4 An example of an elaboration task**

For each of the following superficial elaboration points, develop a more elaborated evaluation.

	Superficial evaluation	Elaborated evaluation
1	Milgram lacked ecological validity	
2	Milgram's research was important	
3	Milgram's study was unethical	

Evaluation toolkits

Like the three-stage model of extended elaboration, thinking toolkits owe much to Vygotskian theory. Vygotsky saw the development of advanced thinking as a process of internalisation of external dialogue to form mental tools. From this perspective, achievement of higher-level thinking in students depends on establishing such dialogue. The rationale for evaluation toolkits is that they provide the basis for such dialogue, which can be internalised to form a set of mental tools for critical thinking. Thinking for a moment in terms of cultural deprivation, this may serve as a leveller, allowing students who have not had the previous experience of such dialogues to compete on a more level playing field with those who, as a function of their social background or educational experiences, are used to thinking in critical terms.

Based on the distinction between analytic and synthetic thinking, McGhee (2001) has offered a set of toolkits for thinking in both ways about psychological theory and research. Thinking analytically involves consideration of ethics, validity, hypothesis derivation, experimental control, etc. Thinking synthetically involves application to real-world situations, identifying unexpected trends in data and consideration of historical and cultural context.

McGhee's toolkits are well worth reading in full, however they are conceptually advanced and aimed at higher-level study. The following toolkits are offered to guide evaluation in post-16 psychology. Box 5.5 shows a toolkit for evaluating studies and Box 5.6 a toolkit for evaluating theories. Both of these include elements of analytic and synthetic thinking, although there is probably little benefit in burdening students with the distinction. The art to using toolkits[1] such as these is to remember that none of these issues will apply equally to every theory and study and to match the salient issue to the material being evaluated. Note also that there is a minimum of technical language in these versions. This is because students with limited understanding tend to use terms like ecological validity, face validity and heuristic value glibly and without elaboration. Withholding these terms until students have mastered their meaning forces them to explain what they mean.

■ Box 5.5 Evaluation of study toolkit

Issue	Cue questions	Student elaborated response
1 Ethics	What ethical issues are raised, e.g. harm, distress, consent, deceit, withdrawal, privacy? Does the importance of results outweigh the cost to participants?	
2 Social sensitivity	Is the whole topic taboo? Do results justify discrimination? Do results suggest something unpleasant about human nature?	
3 Sample	Is overall sample size large? Is sample in each condition large? Is the sample representative?	
4 Environment	Is the environment controlled? Is the environment natural?	
5 Design	Is the design particularly clever? Is there a flaw in the design? Are there inevitable limitations to this type of design, e.g. non-matched groups in natural experiments?	
6 Measures	Are measures of DVs standard or constructed for this study? Do measures seem to be reliable? Do measures seem to be valid?	
7 Theoretical importance	Is the study significant because it provides evidence for or against an important theory?	
8 Practical applications	Does the study have important real-world applications?	

■ **Box 5.6 Evaluation of theory toolkit**

Issue	Cue questions	Student elaborated response
1 Credibility and simplicity	Does the theory make sense? Does it appear to explain a psychological phenomenon? Is there a more obvious explanation that could explain the same data?	
2 Origins	Is the theory built on solid foundations such as good quality research? Is it founded on limited evidence or plucked out of thin air?	
3 Testability	Can any aspects of the theory be tested by psychological studies? Are there parts of the theory that are hard to test by means of psychological studies?	
4 Supporting evidence	Are there studies that support all or part of the theory?	
5 Conflicting evidence	Are there studies that suggest the theory is incorrect?	
6 Completeness	Is there anything important that the theory cannot explain?	
7 Value to psychology	Does the theory help us understand or think about something?	
8 Value to society	Does the theory have practical applications in the real world?	

Repertory techniques

Repertory techniques (Kelly, 1955) are an alternative approach to providing the cues to facilitate higher-level thinking. These come in various formats but share the purpose of making concrete and visible a range of perceptions about an aspect of the world, most commonly a set of interpersonal relationships. These perceptions are called personal constructs. Mayo (2004) has applied the repertory grid technique to helping psychology students analyse psychological theories. The same approach can be used for theory and lends itself to both analysis and evaluation of psychological material. Repertory grids are particularly useful for comparing alternative theories and studies. Examples are shown in Box 5.7.

A limitation of using the traditional binary response format (i.e. yes/no) in repertory grids is that it may encourage unelaborated answers. It can still be a useful starting point, however Mayo suggests that a better response format is a seven-point semantic differential-type rating scale. For example, Milgram's study would be evaluated as shown in Box 5.8.

One of the strengths of repertory techniques, whether in binary form for comparison or in semantic differential form for more in-depth analytical thinking about particular theories or studies, is their potential for use in co-operative learning and for stimulating whole-class discussion. For example, pairs of students can debate where a study falls on each dimension as shown in Box 5.8 then feed their conclusions into a larger discussion. Mayo reports that students surveyed on the use of repertory techniques were enthusiastic and that they were associated with improved test results.

Metacognitive prompts

The techniques reviewed thus far are essentially student-centred. However, there is also a place for whole-class teaching in developing thinking skills. One way of

---

■ **Box 5.7 Use of repertory grids for developing higher-level thinking**

Evaluation of theories of memory

Theories of memory	Credibility/ face validity	Supporting evidence	Conflicting evidence	Complete explanation?	Practical applications
Multistore model	√	√	√	x	√
Levels of processing	√	√	x	x	√
Working memory	√	√	x	x	√

Evaluation of studies of obedience

Studies of obedience	Ethical?	Socially sensitive?	Represent- ative sample	Natural environ- ment	Control	Valid measures	Practical Applications
Milgram	x	√	x	x	√	√	√
Hofling	√	√	x	√	√	√	√
Tarnow	√	√	√	√	x	x	√

■ **Box 5.8 Semantic differential method of evaluation**

Milgram's study is   1   2   3   4   5   6   7

Unethical	←------------------------------→	Ethical
Sensitive	←------------------------------→	Not sensitive
Unrepresentative	←------------------------------→	Representative sample
Unnatural	←------------------------------→	Natural setting
Uncontrolled	←------------------------------→	Well controlled
Invalid	←------------------------------→	Valid measusre
No applications	←------------------------------→	Practical applications

thinking about effective development of thinking during whole-class teaching is in terms of metacognitive prompts. Metacognition is discussed in detail in Chapter 3. Briefly, it refers to our cognitive awareness of our own mental processes. This awareness relies on three types of information: self-knowledge, task knowledge and strategy knowledge. There is a growing consensus among education experts that one of the keys to developing higher-level thinking is to encourage metacognition. The terms we use to give feedback to students can be used to provide cues for metacognitive knowledge. Examples are shown in Table 5.2.

■ **Table 5.2** Teacher prompts to elicit metacognition

Meta-cognitive knowledge	Type of prompt	Example
self	Focus on abilities Focus on learning style Focus on learning strategy Focus on motivational style	'You really enjoy this sort of thinking, don't you?' 'Does seeing it in a table like that make it easier?' 'What do you do when you get homework like this?' 'Do you find it easier in small chunks like this?'
task	Focus on assessment criteria Comparison with other tasks Focus on critical thinking Focus on creative thinking	'What am I looking for when I mark this?' 'What did you find last time we did this?' 'Can you see anything dodgy about that?' 'What can we do about that?'
strategy	Focus on thinking Focus on planning Focus on checking	'Put your thinking cap on for a moment.' 'What's the first thing we have to do?' 'Good. Now look back at what you've done.'

THINKING-BASED MODELS OF PSYCHOLOGY TEACHING

Sternberg's triarchic model

In recent years there has been a growing awareness of the broad range of human mental abilities and a realisation that traditional teaching methods may not always make the best use of these. In response, an enormous number of theories and techniques have emerged. Many of these are simply pop psychology with no empirical basis, and other techniques are based on fundamental misunderstandings of respectable theory. One approach that stands out as having a strong theoretical and empirical basis is Robert Sternberg's triarchic model of teaching. This was developed specifically as a way of teaching introductory psychology, although it has now been successfully employed in a range of subjects and age groups (Grigorenko *et al.*, 2002). The triarchic model seeks to maximise learning by means of employing three modes of thinking: analytic, synthetic and practical.

- ▨ *Analytic*: to Sternberg this is synonymous with critical thinking and involves breaking down a theory or study in order to identify its strengths and limitations.
- ▨ *Synthetic*: this is used in the same way as in other systems to mean creative thinking.
- ▨ *Practical*: this refers to the application of psychological theory or research to a real-world situation.

The rationale behind triarchic teaching is that students both think triarchically to learn and learn to think triarchically. In other words, by constructing lessons or sets of lessons that involve thinking in these three modes we can both aid learning and develop higher-level thinking skills. From this starting point we can put together lessons and schemes of work that contain a balance between tasks using each of these modes of thinking. Table 5.3 shows a set of cues for tasks that make use of each of the three modes. Box 5.9 shows three examples of how tasks requiring analytic, synthetic and practical thinking can be sequenced in a lesson. Note that in each case the tasks are in different order. There is no requirement in the triarchic model for analytic thinking to precede synthetic, etc.

▨ **Table 5.3** Cues for analytic, synthetic and practical thinking tasks (Adapted from Sternberg, 1999)

Mode of thinking	Examples of cues
analytic	assess, critique, criticize, evaluate, judge, analyse, argue for and against, question the evidence for, defend, debate, compare the contributions of
synthetic	create, design, imagine, combine, put together, formulate a hypothesis
practical	apply, use, implement, put into practice, demonstrate, explain using theory

---

■ **Box 5.9 Three examples of task sequences based on triarchic theory**

1: The debate over day care

■ Explain using attachment theory how long hours in day care in early infancy might have negative effects on an infant's development (requires practical thinking).

■ Assess the strength of the evidence that suggests that day care can have negative effects on infant development (requires analytic thinking).

■ Design a leaflet offering advice to parents considering using day care (requires synthetic thinking).

2: Comparing psychoanalysis and cognitive-behavioural therapy (CBT)

■ Compare the evidence for the effectiveness of analysis and CBT (requires analytic thinking).

■ Put together some principles of psychoanalysis and CBT and come up with your own therapy (requires synthetic thinking).

■ Bernard has come to therapy seeking help for his lack of confidence in meeting women. Use the principles of psychoanalysis and CBT to explain why he might have this problem and what can be done to help him (requires practical thinking).

3: Eyewitness testimony

■ Based on your knowledge of past studies, design your own study of eyewitness testimony that we can carry out in class (requires synthetic thinking).

■ Explain using theories of memory and forgetting why eyewitness testimony might be inaccurate (requires practical thinking)

■ Assess the usefulness of eyewitness testimony as a source of evidence in the classroom (requires analytic thinking).

There is a small but respectable body of research to suggest that the triarchic approach is an effective approach to lesson planning. Sternberg and Clinkenbeard (1995) assessed 199 American college students for their preferences for critical, creative and practical thinking and designed a course in introductory psychology that either corresponded or failed to correspond to these preferences. When assessed, students whose learning activities had been congruent with their preferences did significantly better, supporting the idea – central to triarchic theory – that individuals have strengths and weaknesses across the three domains. Sternberg *et al.* (1998) went on to compare a triarchic model of teaching with a traditional memory-based model of teaching and a critical thinking model, which focused on critical evaluation of material without creative or practical tasks. A total of 141 American high school children were taught introductory psychology at a university summer school in three groups. One was memory-based, emphasising information-processing strategies for learning psychological material. The second was critical thinking-based and the third was taught triarchically. Assessments showed that the triarchic group did best, followed by the critical thinking group and finally the memory-based group.

The four-question model

More recently Dietz-Uhler and Lanter (2009) have proposed a four-question model for maximising the depth and range of information processing during student learning. The four questions are intended to encourage four different deep-level thinking processes:

■ analysis of the material
■ reflection on it
■ relating the material to an aspect of the student's life
■ generation of one or more questions about the material

The four questions used by Dietz-Uhler and Lanter are shown in Box 5.10.

In the original study students were asked to generate around 100 words for each of the first three questions. You might want to vary this according to how challenging you think your students will find the task and how much time you want to invest in the exercise.

The four-question technique has been demonstrated to improve retention of material. Dietz-Uhler and Lanter were initially interested in undergraduate teaching, however they suggested that the technique should be applicable across a range of subjects and levels. The technique has been successfully trialled with A-level students. Kuwar (2010) found that asking the four questions in relation to abnormal psychology led to significantly better performance on a quiz. Students also rated the four-question technique as a valuable learning tool.

CONCLUSIONS AND REFLECTIONS

It is now widely acknowledged that developing thinking skills is an important aspect of education and that the discipline of psychology requires the development of particular modes of thinking. The A-level curriculum is based on Bloom's taxonomy of basic and higher thinking skills, marked as AO1 and AO2. A common criticism of post-16 teaching from both HE teachers and A-level examiners is that there is a tendency for students to learn over-simple and formulaic strategies for

---

■ **Box 5.10 Dietz-Uhler and Lanter's four questions**

1 Identify one important concept, research finding, theory, or idea in psychology that you learned while completing this activity
2 Why do you believe that this concept, research finding, theory, or idea in psychology is important?
3 Apply what you have learned from this activity to some aspect of your life
4 What question(s) has the activity raised for you? What are you still wondering about?

gaining AO2 marks, often missing opportunities to develop genuine higher-level thinking abilities.

An important distinction in understanding psychological thinking is between analytic and synthetic modes of thinking. There are a number of strategies that can be used to develop analytic and synthetic thinking. This is likely to benefit students both in their post-16 achievements and in more advanced study. Such methods include AO2 evaluation, the use of evaluation toolkits and repertory techniques, and peer evaluation. For planning whole lessons, Sternberg has put forward a model of psychology teaching based on sequencing tasks of analytic, synthetic and practical thinking. The four-question model supplements this by providing a way of stimulating a range of deep information processing of psychological material. The evidence base for these strategies is small but respectable. It does seem then that it is possible to develop higher-level thinking in psychology students, but that it probably requires going beyond traditional teaching methods.

QUESTIONS FOR REFLECTION

1 Why are thinking skills important?
2 How much do you do to promote psychological thinking in the classroom?
3 To what extent is psychological thinking scientific thinking?
4 Compare two classroom exercises that might be used to enhance critical thinking skills.
5 How could you plan lessons using the triarchic model and/or the four-question model?

NOTE

1   Feel free to copy and use these pro formas but please credit me in any publications.

FURTHER READING

Kuwar, B. (2010) Using the four-question technique in A-level psychology to enhance learning. *e-Journal of Psychology Teaching* **1**, 8–15.

McGhee, P. (2001) *Thinking psychologically.* Basingstoke, Palgrave. http://www.patrickmcghee.co.uk

Sternberg, R.J., Torff, B. and Grigorenko, E.L. (1998) Teaching triarchically improves school achievement. *Journal of Educational Psychology* **90**, 1–11.

Tombs, S. (2004) Writing, arguing and evaluation – the perspective from Higher Education. *Psychology Teaching* Summer 2004, 36–8.

CHAPTER 6

RESOURCING THE TEACHING OF PSYCHOLOGY

By the end of this chapter you should be able to:

- Outline research into the characteristics of psychology textbooks.
- Consider the impact of a range of textual features and pedagogical aids on learning.
- Apply an understanding of textual features and pedagogical aids to designing student resources.
- Describe the use of newspaper articles to help students apply psychological theory to real life.
- Discuss the use of popular culture to illustrate and demonstrate psychology with particular regard to the portrayal of mental disorder in film and the deconstruction of popular lyrics.
- Understand the benefits of using a range of formats for assessment materials.

All psychology teachers use a range of resources, produced both commercially and in-house, to put across psychological information. These include published textbooks and videos and home-grown handouts and worksheets. They also include a range of resources intended for other purposes and imaginatively adapted for teaching. The aim of this chapter is to help teachers better understand some of the criteria by which existing resources can be evaluated and new ones developed. We are talking here of resources in conventional formats. Chapter 7 deals separately with online and software resources.

PSYCHOLOGY TEXTBOOKS

There is a choice of textbooks available for every post-16 psychology syllabus. It would be inappropriate for several reasons to pick apart particular books or to make recommendations. Perhaps the most obvious research question we can ask about psychology texts is what are they like? There is a tradition in the USA of content-analysing and comparing textbooks. This has been supplemented in the UK by a tradition of more critical qualitative research seeking to identify more subtle dimensions of content such as bias.

Sameness hypothesis

A popular stereotype of psychology texts, especially those produced in the USA, is that they are all pretty much the same. Actually research has shown that this apparent similarity is largely a product of similarity in chapter structures. This has always been the case in the USA where general academic psychology textbooks are most commonly structured around the standard first-year undergraduate course (Psych101). This sort of structural similarity has increased in the UK in the past decade as there has been a move towards following the structure of A-level specifications.

When Jackson *et al.* (2000) reviewed 41 American general introductory psychology texts they found that 39 followed an almost identical structure. However, this says little about the coverage within those structures and so can give a misleading impression of sameness. Zechmeister and Zechmeister (2000) looked at the glossaries of 10 American introductory textbooks published between 1994 and 1997. They found that 49% of key terms only occurred in one text and that only 3% were identified in all 10. In a study of 24 American introductory texts Gorenflo and McConnell (1991) failed to find a single reference that was cited in all books. These studies suggest that even in content textbooks vary considerably.

Perhaps more importantly there is also considerable variation in the sort of text features used in different books (Marek *et al.*, 1999) – the only feature shared by all analysed texts being emboldened terms. Clearly then, not all psychology textbooks are the same. This does not mean, of course, that there are necessarily substantial differences in quality, merely that each writer represents psychology as they see it and uses the sort of chapter features they believe to be pedagogically useful. When you are choosing a book or books for your students you might want to consider which representation of psychology and which pedagogical aids you prefer for your students. There is always a healthy debate around Internet forums about the merits of different books, but remember that you know the needs of your particular students best and are better placed to make a judgement than colleagues in different contexts. Also, ask your students for their impressions of different books. Different generations use books differently, and variables that you might not have thought about can make all the difference to whether students engage with a book. As Griggs and Marek (2001) say, careful choice of textbooks is a worthwhile investment of teacher time.

Qualitative critiques of psychology texts

While American textbook research has focused on their quantitative dimensions, qualitative studies in the UK have looked at the more subtle dimensions of psychology texts. Howitt and Owusu-Bempah (1994) focused on the use of racist language, exemplified by the use of the word 'tribe' in a leading American text. Words like 'tribe' are considered racist, because the term can refer both to humans and animals, but when referring to humans is almost always used to refer to black rather than white people. It thus positions black people as closer to animals than to white people.

In similar vein, Jarvis (2000) has deconstructed the language used to describe Freud in another leading American psychology text. Numerous examples were found of ways in which language could be used to bias a reader against a theory. For example, the sentence 'Although Freud's current influence in psychological science is slight, his notoriety continues to colour people's perceptions of psychology, and his influence lingers in literary interpretation, psychiatry and pop-psychology' can be unpacked in a number of ways. Freud is being associated here with three out-groups, a rival discipline (psychiatry), an inferior discipline (pop psychology) and an irrelevant discipline (literary interpretation). The terms 'notoriety' and 'lingers' are also significant in constructing Freud as an unwelcome and perhaps even criminal influence on psychology. The term 'psychological science' – not used consistently throughout the book – further serves to remind the reader that psychology is a science, and that Freud does not live up to the standards of science.

Pennington (2000) analysed a range of American introductory texts with regard to their claims to support critical thinking (see Chapter 5 for a discussion of critical thinking). All ten texts claimed in their preface to encourage critical thinking, seven giving an explicit definition. The developmental psychology sections were then looked at closely in order to assess how effectively devices were used to encourage critical thinking. The following weaknesses were noted:

▪ In some cases critical thinking questions were asked for which there was little or no relevant material in the text.
▪ Some questions were extremely vague and unclear.
▪ Some questions required value judgements or application rather than critical thinking. This is still higher-level thinking but not critical thinking as defined in the books.
▪ Where sections of critical thinking are included in the text, the work is done and an opportunity is not provided for students to think for themselves.

There are clear lessons from this study, both for teachers looking for effective textbooks and for those looking to devise resources with which to promote critical thinking. Students need to be given the tools with which to think about the material and appropriate material about which to think, but probably not the answers, at least in elaborated form. See p78 for a discussion of strategies to encourage higher-level thinking.

Textbook study guides

Many modern textbooks come with an accompanying study or companion guide. This typically contains advice on how to study, breakdowns and summaries of syllabus material and self-assessments using a variety of formats. In the USA it is common practice to make psychology study guides required reading. As Dickson *et al.* (2005) point out, there are good reasons in terms of information-processing theory to believe that study guides will be helpful; they require students to 'effortfully process and manipulate course material' (Dickson *et al.*: p34), and contain self-assessment questions the use of which is likely to maximise retrieval routes. Dickson *et al.* assessed the effectiveness of study guides with 236 undergraduate psychology students. In one condition students worked with a study guide and in the other a control group completed the same course without the guide. Those using the study guide did better on multiple-choice exams, and when surveyed, most students reported that they found study guides useful and would use them again. Cautiously then, evidence does seem to support the usefulness of study guides.

A word about endorsement

At the time of writing there is a growing trend for Awarding Bodies to endorse textbooks, sometimes, though not always, in exchange for a royalty or commission. This has both potential benefits and costs. On the plus side, at the point of publication an endorsed book will have been quality-assured by the awarding body. Someone will have made a thorough check that the book addresses the specification, and this can give you a sense of security, particularly as a new teacher or one new to teaching psychology. However, be aware of some limitations of the endorsement process:

■ Although endorsed texts are rigorously reviewed before publication this is standard practice across the industry, and all published texts will have had feedback from someone very familiar with the specification and its assessment.

■ Specifications and assessment practices develop after publication. The fact that a textbook was rigorously checked on publication does not guarantee that it will still equip students for their exams two or three years down the line.

■ Many writers and publishers do not seek endorsement, and publishers may fail in bids for endorsement on purely commercial grounds. Non-endorsed products have not been rejected for endorsement, and you cannot therefore use endorsement as an objective way to distinguish between products of different quality.

■ Endorsement deals may be done at any stage in the writing process. Sometimes this means that a deal is struck because a book is complete and clearly fit for purpose. However, depending on the practices of your Awarding Body, it may also be the case that a deal is done on commercial grounds before writers are even recruited. Here there is very little reason to suppose that an endorsed book will have any advantage over other products.

This isn't a polemic against endorsement, just a note of caution. Choose the book or books that, all things considered, you think best meet the needs of your students. Remember as well that all resources, free or paid for, endorsed or not, are provided in good faith but without any guarantee that they will satisfy all future exam questions. Textbook coverage is not and will never be the criterion on which exam questions are set.

TEXTUAL CHARACTERISTICS AND PEDAGOGICAL AIDS

What makes a good resource?

Clearly students need to be able to concentrate on, understand and remember text before it becomes a useful resource. There are a number of variables that can affect how easy a piece of text is to process. These range from the physical layout of the page, use of figures and pictures etc. to the ways words are put together and the use of various pedagogical aids.

Page layout

This is an area plagued by poor-quality research and misguided attempts to apply findings from one culture and age group to others. Studies of font readability, for example, have often not controlled for letter height, line spacing or density of text on the page, all of which are confounding variables, and which the writer can alter. As in all things, do what works for you and your students rather than follow the dogma. The following suggestions are intended as some ideas worth trying, but I stress that they are based on limited empirical research.

- Try increasing line spacing slightly and compensate by taking the font size down a fraction. Several studies have found that line spacing is more important than font size in making text readable. An example is shown in Box 6.1.
- Try using unjustified text. This can make your resource look a little less slick but again research tends to find that unjustified text is easier to read. An example is shown in Box 6.2.
- Try inserting images into the text. Some studies have shown that students with a more visual style of information processing (see Chapter 8 for a critical discussion of learning styles) find text easier to process if there are images present. An example is shown in Box 6.3.

■ **Box 6.1 The effect of varying font size and line spacing: which of these is easier to read?**

Example 1. Times New Roman size 12, line space at 1 point

Bowlby noted that infants are born with a set of instinctive behaviours including smiling, sucking, gesturing and crying. He proposed that these have evolved in order to maximise the chances of being well looked after and hence surviving. Bowlby called these behaviours *social releasers*. Their function is to elicit instinctive parenting responses from adults. The interplay between social releasers and parenting responses is the process that builds the attachment between infant and carer.

Example 2. Times New Roman size 11.5, line space at 0.6cm

Bowlby noted that infants are born with a set of instinctive behaviours including smiling, sucking, gesturing and crying. He proposed that these have evolved in order to maximise the chances of being well looked after and hence surviving. Bowlby called these behaviours *social releasers*. Their function is to elicit instinctive parenting responses from adults. The interplay between social releasers and parenting responses is the process that builds the attachment between infant and carer.

■ **Box 6.2 The effect of unjustified text: which of these is easier to read?**

Example 1. Justified

Bowlby noted that infants are born with a set of instinctive behaviours including smiling, sucking, gesturing and crying. He proposed that these have evolved in order to maximise the chances of being well looked after and hence surviving. Bowlby called these behaviours social releasers. Their function is to elicit instinctive parenting responses from adults. The interplay between social releasers and parenting responses is the process that builds the attachment between infant and carer.

Example 2. Unjustified

Bowlby noted that infants are born with a set of instinctive behaviours including smiling, sucking, gesturing and crying. He proposed that these have evolved in order to maximise the chances of being well looked after and hence surviving. Bowlby called these behaviours social releasers. Their function is to elicit instinctive parenting responses from adults. The interplay between social releasers and parenting responses is the process that builds the attachment between infant and carer.

■ **Box 6.3 The effect of adding an image: which of these is easier to read?**

Example 1. Without image

Bowlby noted that infants are born with a set of instinctive behaviours including smiling, sucking, gesturing and crying. He proposed that these have evolved in order to maximise the chances of being well looked after and hence surviving. Bowlby called these behaviours social releasers. Their function is to elicit instinctive parenting responses from adults. The interplay between social releasers and parenting responses is the process that builds the attachment between infant and carer.

Example 2. With image

Bowlby noted that infants are born with a set of instinctive behaviours including smiling, sucking, gesturing and crying. He proposed that these have evolved in order to maximise the chances of being well looked after and hence surviving. Bowlby called these behaviours social releasers. Their function is to elicit instinctive parenting responses from adults. The interplay between social releasers and parenting responses is the process that builds the attachment between infant and carer.

Text readability

How easy a piece of text is to read varies in line with several dimensions of the way it is worded. There are a range of formulae around from which a readability index can be calculated. Typically these input variables such as sentence length, number of letters per word and number of syllables per word. For example the Fog Index is calculated using the following formula.

Index = 0.4 (words/sentences+100(words >2 syllables/words))

There are interactive websites that will calculate your readability indices for you. I recommend readability.info (http://www.readability.info/), because this gives scores using several different formulae and also reports on other variables that might impact on readability. These include the following:

■ Use of the passive voice can make text harder to follow.
■ Conjunctions lengthen sentences and may make them harder to follow.
■ Too many pronouns can make meaning ambiguous, however too few tend to lead it to lack fluidity.

Box 6.4 shows how a piece of text of mine fares when analysed for readability. From the breakdown of the high Fog Index in Box 6.4 it seems that the problem is the number of long words. Box 6.5 shows the same text rewritten with the number of three-syllable words reduced. The Fog Index is now 10.8, within acceptable limits.

■ **Box 6.4 Readability of a text extract from Jarvis (2001)** *Angles on child psychology*

Bowlby noted that infants are born with a set of instinctive behaviours including smiling, sucking, gesturing and crying. He proposed that these have evolved in order to maximise the chances of being well looked after and hence surviving. Bowlby called these behaviours *social releasers*. Their function is to elicit instinctive parenting responses from adults. The interplay between social releasers and parenting responses is the process that builds the attachment between infant and carer.

Fog Index = 14.6. The ideal is 7–8. A score of over 12 indicates that most people would find it hard to read.

0 long sentences. 2 short sentences. Words >2 syllables = 14 Average syllables = 1.68

■ **Box 6.5 Readability of a modified text extract**

Bowlby noted that infants are born with a set of behaviours such as smiling, sucking, waving and crying. He proposed that these have evolved in order to improve the chances of being well looked after and hence living to adulthood. Bowlby called these behaviours *social releasers*. Their function is to trigger innate parenting responses from adults. The exchange of social releasers and adult responses is the process that builds the attachment between infant and carer.

Fog Index = 10.8

Words > 2 syllables = 9 Average syllables = 1.53

Making textual changes: coherence and linking

Although it can be very instructive to submit both your own handouts and the textbooks you use to readability analysis, there are other variables to take into account and a readability index does not tell the whole story. Vidal-Abarca and Sanjose (1998) suggest two ways to enhance the readability of text that would not show up on a readability analysis. These are coherence textual changes and linking textual changes. *Coherence* textual changes involve improving the overall coherence of a passage, for example by adding headings and summaries, and by linking one idea to another. *Linking* textual changes involve explicitly linking new ideas to the reader's existing knowledge. Consider the passage in Box 6.6.

▨ Box 6.6 A passage including coherence and linking changes

Vygotsky was writing at around the time of Piaget's early work. ◄─── Linking textual change

Like Piaget he believed that cognitive development occurs in stages and that each stage involves qualitatively different thinking abilities. However his theory differed in several key ways.

Coherence textual change ───►

The importance of culture and social interaction

Vygotsky placed far more emphasis than did Piaget on the role played by culture in the child's development. Vygotsky saw ◄─── Linking textual change

children as being born with basic mental functions such as the ability to perceive the outside world and to focus attention on particular objects. However, children lack higher mental functions such as thinking and problem solving. These higher mental functions are seen as cultural 'tools'. Tools are trans-mitted to children by older members of the culture in guided learning experiences (such as lessons in school), and include the ability to use language, art and mathematics. Experiences with other people gradually become internalised and form the child's internal representation of the world.

Coherence textual change ───►

The Zone of Proximal Development

In contrast to Piaget, who emphasised how much a child can learn by exploring its environment, Vygotsky put his emphasis on the fact that children can develop their under-standing far more quickly whilst interacting with other people. Children, according to Vygotsky, could never develop formal operational thinking without the help of others. The difference between what a child can understand on its own and what it can potentially understand through interaction with others is called the Zone of Proximal Development (ZPD).

The role of language

Vygotsky placed far more emphasis on the importance of language in cognitive development than did Piaget. For Piaget, ◄─── Linking textual change

language simply appeared when the child had reached a suffi-ciently advanced stage of development. The child's grasp of language depended on its current level of cognitive develop-ment. For Vygotsky however language developed from social interactions with others and was a very important cultural tool. At first the sole function of language is communication, and language and thought develop separately. Later, the child internalises language and learns to use it as a tool of thinking

Coherence textual change ───►

Summary

Vygotsky emphasised the role of interaction with others in cognitive development, seeing higher mental processes as acquired from other people. He saw the limiting factor in development at any time as the presence or absence of a tutor. Language is an important mental tool internalised in contact with others and used for thinking

In Box 6.6, which introduces Vygotsky's theory of cognitive development, it can be seen that coherence is achieved by means of subheadings and a summary section. Linking is achieved by means of references to Piaget, with whom the reader is already familiar.

Emphasising key concepts: signalling and elaboration

Key concepts in a piece of text are said to be *signalled* when they are extracted and explained in detail in boxes. An example is shown in Box 6.7.

Nevid and Lampmann (2003) investigated the effectiveness of signalling. A group of 80 college students read matched textbook passages with or without key terms boxes. They were then tested on the material. Performance in the tests was better overall in the signalled condition. This was accounted for entirely by enhanced performance on the signalled areas, and there was no difference in test performance in the non-signalled content. This supports the usefulness of signalling.

Whenever key terms are defined, irrespective of whether they are signalled, we tend to elaborate on a definition, for example by paraphrasing it, giving an example or providing a mnemonic device to make it more memorable. Balch (2005) compared the usefulness of different types of elaboration in an experiment conducted on first-year American psychology undergraduates. Participants received passages including definitions of 16 psychological terms, followed by either a paraphrase (for example, 'a dissociative disorder is a psychological problem in which people may not remember certain events that happen to them or who they are'), an example (for example, 'a person with a dissociative disorder might be found standing by the road somewhere without knowing how he got there, what is name is or where he lives'), a mnemonic (for example, 'the first

---

■ **Box 6.7 An example of signalling**

Bowlby noted that infants are born with a set of instinctive behaviours including smiling, sucking, gesturing and crying. He proposed that these have evolved in order to maximise the chances of being well looked after and hence surviving. Bowlby called these behaviours *social releasers*. Their function is to elicit instinctive parenting responses from adults. The interplay between social releasers and parenting responses is the process that builds the attachment between infant and carer.

---

1 Key term: social releasers

Instinctive behaviours including smiling and gesturing, designed to elicit nurturing behaviour from adults

---

two syllables of dissociative sound like disco. Discos are usually dark, and people with dissociative disorder are in the dark because of disruptions in the memory, consciousness or identity') or a repeated definition. They were then tested on the terms using multiple-choice questions. Examples and mnemonics were associated with improved performance on the test, however paraphrases and repeated definitions were not.

Comparing pedagogical aids

Gurung (2003) identified seven pedagogical aids commonly used in psychology textbooks. All of these can be used in teacher-generated resources:

- chapter outlines
- chapter summaries
- emboldened terms
- italicised terms
- key terms
- practice questions
- quizzes.

Gurung questioned students about how often they made use of each of these aids and how useful they found them. Emboldened and italicised terms to make important terms stand out and quizzes and practice questions to help test learning were rated as the most helpful and commonly used features. Interestingly though, in a follow-up study, it emerged that the use of such aids declined during a psychology course, suggesting that students may have initially overestimated their usefulness (Gurung, 2004).

A checklist for assessing resources

Given how many variables appear to have an effect on how friendly psychological text is to students, whether in the form of a textbook or teacher-generated handouts, it is worth having a tool with which to examine such resources, in particular your own, which can be easily altered. This is not to suggest that all your resources should use all these devices all the time, just that if you are looking to improve them these ideas might provide ways forward. In that spirit I offer a check-list of text features and pedagogical aids. This is shown in Box 6.8.

RESOURCES THAT APPLY PSYCHOLOGY TO LIFE

News stories

In Chapter 3 I suggested that learning can be improved by making it directly relevant to the lives of students, and that one way in which this can be achieved

■ **Box 6.8 A checklist to assess text features and pedagogical aids in student resources**

Page layout	Font size and line spacing are optimised	Text is unjustified	Images or diagrams are included	
Textual features	Fog Index is <12	Subheadings are used	Summaries are used	Links are made to prior learning
Pedagogical aids	Key terms are emboldened or italicised	Key terms are signalled	Key terms are elaborated	Questions are included

is by the use of articles from the press. Using contrived articles that only tenuously link to the psychology syllabus is probably counterproductive, but regular manual searches of the news are very labour-intensive. One way to locate news stories quickly and easily is by means of Internet searches. This has the additional advantage that text can be quickly cut and pasted into a worksheet, making the exercise an efficient use of teacher time. Some examples of sites that can be used for locating news are shown in Table 6.1.

One way of using news articles in student resources is to follow the text of the article up with a set of questions that encourage the reader to apply particular theories or research findings to explain what happens in the story. An example is shown in Box 6.9.

■ **Table 6.1** Some sources for psychology-related news

Site	Description	Current URL
Psyseek	links to *New York Times* psychology news	http://www.psyseek.co.uk
Google News	searchable news search engine	http://news.google.co.uk
BBC	searchable news site	http://www.bbc.co.uk
Psycport (APA news)	psychology news site	http://www.psycport.com/
Yahoo Science News	searchable science news site	http://uk.news.yahoo.com/505/
The Observer	searchable news site	http://www.guardian.co.uk/

■ **Box 6.9 An example of using a news story as stimulus material in study of destructive obedience**

'Do as you're told' By Nicci Gerrard. From *The Observer Review* 12 October, 1997

CP Snow wrote that 'more hideous crimes have been committed in the name of obedience than have ever been committed in the name of rebellion'.

In the early hours of 13 July 1942, the 500 men of the German Reserve Police Force Battalion 101 – middle-aged family men, too old for the army, barely trained and stationed in Poland – were addressed by their leader, Commander Trapp. In a voice shaky with distress he told them of their next assignment: to seek out and kill the 1800 women and children in the nearby village of Jozefow. Then, astonishingly Trapp told them he knew what a repugnant task some might find it, and that anyone could stand out with no punishment and no reprisals. Out of 500, only 12 men stood out.

During that terrible day, a further 10–20% managed to evade their duty; many more became distressed but continued to carry out the orders. Quite a few exhibited no signs of distress. A few seemed to enjoy themselves.

We are necessarily bred into obedience the moment we are born. How else does a society operate? Politeness and embarrassment are important factors, as is the unwillingness to let someone down. The absorption in the technical aspects of the task makes us lose our sense of what we are doing. We easily fool ourselves that we are not to blame – divesting ourselves of authority and attributing it to a legitimate authority, so that we become a simple agent: 'I was just doing my job'.

Questions

1   What similarities can you see between the responses of the men of Battalion 101 and those of participants in Milgram's procedure?

2   What aspects of the story suggest that some of the men went into an agentic state?

3   One possible weakness of Milgram's theory of obedience is that it does not explain individual differences in behaviour. What individual differences in behaviour can you see here and how do they affect your assessment of Milgram's explanation?

Popular culture: from film to lyrics

There are a number of ways in which popular culture can be brought into the psychology classroom and used to enthuse students. The obvious approach is to show films containing psychologically relevant content. Green (2005) suggests that there are three good reasons to use film in teaching psychology:

■   It allows teachers to make the same point in different ways, serving as an elaboration of the material covered in lessons.

■   It makes psychological material directly relevant to real life and allows us to talk to students in their own language about aspects of their own culture.

■   It can be used to develop critical thinking as students learn to debunk inaccurate portrayals of psychological topics in film.

Green offers the following advice to psychology teachers considering using film as a teaching aid:

■   Watch the film in advance to check that it is relevant and does not contain offensive material.
■   Watch the film with the class.
■   Be aware of copyright laws.
■   Don't feel obliged to watch a long film in full when only a section is of direct relevance.
■   When a film takes a whole lesson follow it with a piece of related homework so that momentum is not lost by the next lesson.

Blair-Broeker (2002) adds an additional piece of advice – be very wary of the phrase 'based on the true story'. There is always a degree of artistic licence in the way films are put together. For example, *A beautiful mind*, the touching story of brilliant mathematician John Nash's struggle with schizophrenia, contains entirely made-up elements that detract from the accurate portrayal of Nash's case and schizophrenia in general. A related issue concerns thinking carefully about what point you are using film to illustrate. Blair-Broeker gives the example of *Sybil*, a film based on a case of dissociative identity disorder (DID, formerly multiple personality disorder). *Sybil* is sometimes used to portray the nature of DID, however, as Blair-Broeker points out, the content of *Sybil* best illustrates the constructive nature of memory and the power of therapist suggestions, thus the best use of *Sybil* in teaching is perhaps as an illustration of the debate over DID as a real disorder. Table 6.2 shows some examples of films useful for illustrating psychological material. This is adapted from Burden (1993), Blair-Broeker (2002) and Green (2005), and is intended to be illustrative rather than exhaustive.

Television also provides opportunities to illustrate psychological material. Although often less profound and moving than feature-length films, TV episodes have the advantages that they are short and convenient. Table 6.3 shows examples of psychological material exemplified in *The Simpsons*.

Film and TV are not the only media in which popular culture lends itself to psychology teaching. For those who teach prejudice and look at discursive or social constructionist approaches, deconstructing the lyrics of some contemporary music is a way to demonstrate the ubiquity of prejudice in language. A published study to use as a demonstration comes from Burns (1998), who deconstructed the lyrics to 'Barbie Girl'. Using this as a starting point, students can deconstruct their own choice of lyrics. There are several Internet sites (e.g. http://www.lyrics.com) where suitable lyrics can easily be obtained. Thinking a bit less deeply for a moment you can have a bit of fun with quizzes that require matching of music to

■ **Table 6.2** Examples of films with themes relevant to psychology

Film	Area of psychology	Psychological material illustrated
Monty Python and the Holy Grail	Defining abnormality	Diagnosis of witchcraft
Sybil	Defining abnormality	Existence of dissociative identity disorder
One Flew Over the Cuckoo's Nest	Defining abnormality	Diagnosis as social control
As Good As It Gets	Psychopathology	Obsessive compulsive disorder
Born on the 4th of July	Psychopathology	Post-traumatic stress
Rainman	Psychopathology	High functioning autistic spectrum disorder
A Beautiful Mind	Psychopathology	Schizophrenia
Fight Club	Psychopathology	Dissociative identity disorder
Nurse Betty	Psychopathology	Dissociative fugue
Hamlet	Psychopathology	Depression
The Horse Whisperer	Psychopathology	Depression
Henry Portrait of a Serial Killer	Psychopathology	Antisocial personality disorder
Silence of the Lambs	Psychopathology	Antisocial personality disorder
I Am Sam	Psychopathology	Retardation
Analyse This	Psychoanalysis	Psychoanalytic psychotherapy
Star Wars	Psychoanalysis	Oedipus Complex and Jungian archetypes
The Forbidden Planet	Psychoanalysis	Id/superego conflict
Memento	Memory	Anterograde amnesia
Total Recall	Memory	Retrograde amnesia
Boys Don't Cry	Relationships/homophobia	Treatment of a young lesbian
Gregory's Girl	Adolescence	Adolescent relationships
Rebel Without a Cause	Adolescence	Adolescent identity
American Beauty	Adult development	Midlife crisis
Alive and Kicking	Addiction	Heroin addiction
The Basketball Diaries	Addiction	Heroin addiction
Awakenings	Neurological disorder	Sleeping sickness
My Own Private Idaho	Neurological disorder	Narcolepsy
The Experiment	Social psychology	Group processes and tyranny

psychological studies, theories or concepts. Table 6.4 gives examples of suitable songs to match up with the core studies of OCR AS psychology.

Quizzes like this are relatively easy to make up now because of free online databases like Spotify. These are searchable so just put in keywords and you will find a selection of songs. It is very straightforward to put together a playlist for your quiz and store it online.

■ **Table 6.3** Psychological themes in *The Simpsons*

Episode	Title	Psychological theme
Series 1 episode 2	Bart the Genius	Adjustment of children with high IQ
Series 1 episode 5	Bart the General	Bullying at school
Series 1 episode 6	Moaning Lisa	Depression and sublimation
Series 2 episode 9	Itchy & Scratchy & Marge	Media violence
Series 3 episode 1	Stark raving Dad	Defining abnormality/psychiatric diagnosis
Series 3 episode 18	Separate vocations	Psychometric testing
Series 4 episode 10	Lisa's first words	Language development
Series 4 episode 21	Marge in chains	Kleptomania
Series 5 episode 4	Rosebud	Transitional objects (object relations)
Series 5 episode 9	The last temptation of Homer	Midlife crisis
Series 6 episode 3	Another Simpsons clip show	Relationships
Series 6 episode 8	Lisa on ice	Sibling rivalry
Series 6 episode 10	Grandpa vs sexual inadequacy	Oedipus Complex
Series 6 episode 11	Fear of flying	Phobia of flying
Series 6 episode 24	Lemon of Troy	Robbers Cave experiment spoof
Series 7 episode 23	Much Apu about nothing	Racism
Series 8 episode 15	Homer's phobia	Homophobia
Series 9 episode 13	The joy of sect	Cults
Series 10 episode 2	The wizard of Evergreen Terrace	Midlife crisis
Series 10 episode 16	Make room for Lisa	Territoriality
Series 11 episode 2	Brother's little helper	ADHD
Series 13 episode 5	The blunder years	Recovered memories
Series 14 episode 16	The wandering juvie	Adolescence

ASSESSMENT MATERIALS

A further category of resources that has not yet been mentioned is assessment materials. Clearly it is very important to familiarise students with the type of assessment materials they will come across in exams. However there are benefits to using a variety of assessment formats:

■ Varying assessment formats can help keep student interest.

■ Varying formats can also cater for students with a range of information-processing styles.

■ Varying assessment formats may also maximise retrieval routes, making material more memorable (Dickson *et al.*, 2005).

■ **Table 6.4** A songs quiz for OCR AS psychology

Study	Artist	Song
Loftus and Palmer	Snow Patrol	*Headlights on Dark Roads*
Baron-Cohen *et al.*	Kylie Minogue	*In Your Eyes*
Savage-Rumbaugh	Jesus and Mary Chain	*Some Candy Talking*
Milgram	Dean Martin	*Baby Obey Me*
Reicher and Haslam	Mariah Carey	*Prisoner*
Piliavin *et al.*	The Jam	*Down in the Tube Station*
Freud	Morrissey	*The Father Who Must Be Killed*
Samuel and Bryant	Dinosaur Jr	*Not the Same*
Bandura *et al.*	Peaches	*Hit It*
Thigpen and Cleckley	All About Eve	*Wild Hearted Woman*
Rosenhan	Cheap Trick	*Voices*
Griffiths	The Ting Tings	*Fruit Machine*
Sperry	Percy Sledge	*Out of Left Field*
Dement and Kleitman	Susan Boyle	*I Dreamed a Dream*
Maguire	Lenny Kravitz	*Mr. Cab Driver*

Some of the common assessment formats are as follows:

■ essays
■ short answer questions
■ multiple choice
■ cloze
■ crossword
■ true–false.

Each of these formats is demonstrated below, and they are then compared. Each is concerned with the topic of obedience.

1   *Essay*
    Critically discuss two studies of obedience.

2   *Short answer question*

    (a)   Describe the procedure of Milgram's classic study of obedience. (4)
          ....
          ....
          ....

    (b)   Outline Milgram's findings. (4)
          ....
          ....
          ....

(c)　Critically consider the ethics of Milgram's study. (4)

....

....

....

3　*Multiple choice*

(a)　Milgram's participants were:
a. children　b. men　c. women　d. men and women　e. dogs

(b)　Mr Wallace is best described as a
a. stooge　　b. Iggy　c. stodge　d. stoolpigeon　　e. stirrer

(c)　The percentage of participants that gave 300 volts was
a. 0%　　b. 10%　c. 25%　　d. 65%　　e. 100%

(d)　The percentage of participants that gave 450 volts was
a. 0%　　b. 10%　c. 25%　　d. 65%　　e. 100%

(e)　Which was the most common reaction of participants
a. distress　b. joy　c. sadness　d. amusement　e. indifference

4.　*Cloze*

Milgram advertised for _____ volunteers to take part in a memory experiment for a fee of $4. When the 40 participants arrived at the university, the participants were told they would be either a teacher or a learner. They were then introduced to 'Mr _____,' a mild-mannered middle-aged man as a fellow participant (in fact he was a stooge). By fiddling an apparently random procedure, Milgram ensured that the participant was always the _____ and 'Mr Wallace' was always the _____. Mr Wallace was then strapped into a chair and given a memory task involving remembering pairs of words. Every time Wallace made a mistake Milgram ordered the participant to give him an _____ _____. Of course there were no real shocks, but there was no way for the participant to realise this. Following each mistake the level of the 'shock' appeared to increase. The shock levels on the machine were labelled from 0–450 volts and also had signs saying 'danger – severe shock' and, at 450 volts XXX. Milgram ordered participants to continue giving increased shocks whilst the learner shouted and screamed in pain then appeared to collapse. When participants protested Milgram told them 'the experiment requires that you continue'. To Milgram's surprise, all the participants gave Mr Wallace at least _____ (more than you would receive from the mains supply in Britain), and ___% went the distance, giving the full 450 volts to an apparently dead Mr Wallace. Most of the participants protested and some wept and begged in their distress, obviously believing that they had killed Mr Wallace.

5. *Crossword*

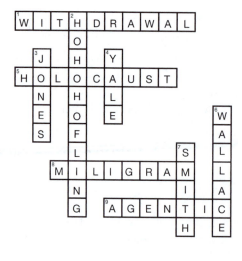

Across

1. WITHDRAWAL—Milgram denied people this right when he told them they must continue
5. HOLOCAUST—Milgram's experiment was inspired by this
8. MILIGRAM—Lightweight obedience researcher
9. AGENTIC—state in which we obey – think Bond

Down

2. HOHOHOFLING—obedience researcher or a quick romp with Santa
3. JONES—The stooge patient in Hofling's study
4. YALE—The university where Milgram did his research
6. WALLACE—Not Mel Gibson, Milgram's stooge
7. SMITH—The doctor in Hofling's study

■ **Figure 6.1** Crossword as assessment material

6. *True–false*

Identify each of the following statements as either true or false.

a. Milgram's participants were working class men	TRUE	FALSE
b. Mr Wallace was one of the participants	TRUE	FALSE
c. There were 60 participants in the original study	TRUE	FALSE
d. 100% of participants gave Mr Wallace 450V	TRUE	FALSE
e. Most participants were unhappy but obeyed Milgram	TRUE	FALSE

One thing to bear in mind is that different assessments rely on different aspects of memory; exam essays are tests of free recall, providing few cues. This means that students need to learn to write essay plans in order to cue themselves as they write in exam conditions. Short answer exercises are tests of cued recall and multiple choice and true–false exercises test recognition. Cued recall and recognition are easier than free recall, however these types of question leave no scope for the skilled writer to waffle. Crosswords and related tasks like word searches rely on a quite different type of information processing – what Gregorc (1979) has called random as opposed to sequential processing. This type of exercise often favours students who struggle with more logical sequential tasks, thus they can serve as encouragement for students with more unusual styles of information processing.

CONCLUSIONS AND REFLECTIONS

Psychology teachers constantly select from published resources and develop many of their own. It is therefore very helpful to have a clear understanding of what you think makes a good resource. Textbooks have been the subject of a considerable body of research. No support exists for the sameness hypothesis – psychology texts vary considerably in both their content and use of pedagogical aids. There is a small body of research to suggest that well-constructed study guides can be helpful in supporting students to use textbooks. Understanding effective text is a surprisingly technical business, and it is perhaps worth becoming a bit more familiar with applied linguistics – this deals with aspects of text such as readability, coherence, linking, signalling and elaboration.

Resources are not always in verbal form and perform many functions other than transmitting psychological information. Video and news material can be extremely useful in making psychology relevant to the lives of students. Films can be useful, however TV programmes are often shorter and illustrate the same points in condensed form – *The Simpsons* is particularly useful, illustrating psychological themes from the social consequences of hot-housing to sibling rivalry, media violence, homophobia and the mid-life crisis. Another function of resources is assessment. There are a number of assessment formats, ranging from the traditional essay to crosswords. It is worth being aware of the different implications of these and using a variety of approaches.

QUESTIONS FOR REFLECTION

1   How do you choose textbooks. How might you make this process more scientific?
2   What criticisms can be made of psychology texts? How can you make up for these problems?
3   What text variables may impact on how easy a text is to use.
4   How and when might film and TV be used in psychology lessons?
5   What formats do you use to assess your students? What factors do you take into account when choosing these or putting them together?

FURTHER READING

Blair-Broeker, C. (2002) Bringing psychology to life. *Essays from e-xcellence in teaching* 2, np.
Griggs, R.A. and Marek, P. (2001) Similarity of introductory psychology textbooks: reality or illusion? *Teaching of Psychology* 28, 254–6.
Rose, D. and Radford, J. (1993) *Teaching psychology: information and resources*. Leicester, BPS Books.

CHAPTER 7

TECHNOLOGY-ENHANCED PSYCHOLOGY TEACHING

By the end of this chapter you should be able to:

- Take a view on the potential for information and communication technology (ICT) to enhance teaching and learning.
- Apply some principles of effective learning to teaching with ICT.
- Define some key terms used in relation to ICT and learning.
- Discuss the uses and pitfalls of presentation tools like PowerPoint in the classroom.
- Use online video, 3-D models and simulations to extend the presentation of psychology material.
- Understand the issues around using web-cams for teaching observation and use zoo-cams.
- Understand how to organise search tasks for students.
- Create interactive assessment resources and organise learning resources on a virtual learning environment.
- Appreciate the potential of Web 2.0 technology and use Web 2.0 resources including blogs, wikis and private social networks for teaching purposes.

Technology has numerous possible uses in the psychology classroom. Some areas of practice are covered elsewhere in this book, for example, use of online simulated experiments and statistical analysis software is covered in Chapter 4 in relation to practical work, while making electronic resources more accessible is addressed in Chapter 8 as part of the discussion of meeting diverse student needs. One of the greatest social changes in the early 21st century has been the rapid development of computer-related technology. The importance of ICT (information and communication technology) is growing rapidly and many millions of pounds have been invested in bringing information technology to education. The main aims of this chapter are to try to tease out some of the psychology of what might make ICT of direct benefit to learning, and to look in detail at how a range of ICT-related activities can be carried out. Clearly ICT hardware is expensive and software potentially so. Throughout this chapter the emphasis is on free software and free Internet sites.

POTENTIAL BENEFITS AND PITFALLS OF USING TECHNOLOGY

Recall the discussion of effective teaching in Chapter 1. The importance we place on using ICT depends on our values and priorities about teaching. A highly empathic or brilliantly inspiring teacher should not be censured for not using enough technology, and the evidence linking technology to attainment is inconsistent, varying considerably from one subject to another, with psychology not having been systematically investigated (Machin *et al.*, 2007). However technology undoubtedly has the potential to enhance the quality of student experience. Note the word 'potential' though. When it comes to technology it is very much a case of 'it ain't what you do, it's the way that you do it ... and the time that you do it ... and the place that you do it'. Cognitive-developmental theorist Seymour Papert (1996) has described teachers who favour the traditional classroom and who only cautiously use computers as 'cyberostriches'. I actually worry more about the 'cyberlemming', who rushes into ICT use without consideration of the ways students learn. Good use of ICT is likely to improve your teaching but bad use will certainly make it worse. With that note of caution in mind, let's focus on the positive and look at some benefits of ICT use (adapted from JISC, 2008).

- ■ *Cost and time saving*: a well resourced learning platform can cut down dramatically on preparation time and save on department photocopying costs.
- ■ *Recruitment and retention*: an attractive and well-organised set of electronic resources can aid recruitment and retention of students.
- ■ *Transferable skills*: familiarising students with a range of ICT applications helps develop their ICT skills for the future.
- ■ *Student achievement*: there is some evidence to support the idea that judicious use of technology can benefit students in terms of achievement/attainment.
- ■ *Inclusion*: ICT can be used to present material in ways that are compatible with particular styles of information processing, and online resources make education available to students who cannot attend classes because of health, social circumstances, disability or geographical factors.

Keeping the focus on principles of effective learning

However sophisticated our understanding of the technical side of technology we should always bear in mind that all technology is simply a set of tools, and that what we do with it should conform to principles of effective learning just like any other mode of teaching. Recall from Chapter 3 that, although we would be unwise to come out strongly for or against a particular model of teaching, we can abstract from education research a set of broad principles that underlie effective learning and teaching.

- Learning should be an active process rather than a passive process of taking in information. This is achieved when students use software themselves, for example, searching, presenting, running simulations or analysing data with statistical software.
- Learning should be an interactive process. Interactions take place with the teacher, peers and software. Teacher interaction can be in the form of whole-class discussions following the stimulus of a presentation or of scaffolding search, simulation and data analysis tasks.
- Learning should be made as relevant as possible to the learner. It is all too easy to get lost in search tasks that simply transfer from one metasite to another. ICT tasks must be focused either on bringing psychology to life or on developing course-related knowledge and skills.
- Learning should be memorable in order to prepare for exams. Material tends to be memorable when it has been deeply processed, visualised and when recall has been practised. Software can help with all these provided its use is well planned.

These principles become important when we start to consider some common practices such as using presentation software in the classroom and populating a virtual learning environment (VLE) with handouts. This is not to say that using presentation software or VLE technology is wrong, just that we need to think about it in terms of how learning happens if we want it to impact positively on our students.

The secret language of ICT: is it all Geek to you?

Would you know a Ning from a Spruz or understand what e-learning specialists mean when they meet your reasonable-sounding request for a feature for the school VLE with a shake of the head and a mutter of 'too much server-side scripting'? ICT has not so much its own language as a whole set of languages for different specialisms. One of the things that makes it hard to get to grips with educational ICT is this esoteric language. Historically, this has meant that the overlap between those with a grasp of the technology and those with a good understanding of pedagogy has been very small. This, in turn, meant that in many cases the introduction of ICT to education was driven by the technically minded rather than the pedagogically wise, leading to expensive failures and a degree of teacher resistance. With that in mind here are some of the basics explained.

ICT, ILT & e-learning

There is a basic distinction between information and communication technology (ICT) and information and learning technology (ILT). *ICT* is a generic term used to describe computing hardware and related communication technology such as telephone systems and networked computers. *ILT* is a fairly broad term that denotes 'the application of IT skills to learning situations using ICT' (National Learning Network, 2004, np). In other words, the focus in ILT is on ways in which to use ICT to enhance learning. In the past five years, however, the term ILT has fallen out of favour because it implies an emphasis on the technology rather than on teaching and learning. The term e-learning, which originally referred to the delivery of whole courses online, is now more commonly used as a generic term to mean the use of technology in an educational context.

CAL and CBL

There are a range of philosophies as regards how e-learning should be carried out. In particular, there are debates about the extent to which ICT should fit into the traditional classroom and the extent to which it should shape the learning environments of the future. Broadly, computer-*aided* learning (CAL) takes place in a fairly traditional classroom. This approach is also sometimes called *technology-enhanced learning*. Computer-*based* learning, by contrast, takes place in a computer suite or students' own homes, with most or all activities being done on computers. Currently – although of course this may change – most developments are in the area of computer-aided learning and this is reflected in the emphasis in this chapter.

Intranets, CMSs, VLEs & MLEs

Leafe defines an intranet as 'a web or network-based system open to approved users' (2001: 182). It is really just a section of the Internet to which passwords are required for access. It is now the norm for computers in schools and colleges to be networked. Content may be shared on an intranet by means of a content management system (CMS). Content management systems can generally allow approved users – which may or may not include teachers depending on the institutional culture – to generate web pages, attach files and communicate by e-mail. A virtual learning environment (VLE) is a specialist CMS with education-specific tools for assessment and tracking. VLEs are discussed in more detail on p125. A managed learning environment (MLE) includes a VLE and a management information system (MIS). The MIS is used to track attendance, achievement, etc.

The remainder of this chapter is about practical strategies for using technology to support learning of psychology in the classroom and via the Internet. We are talking here about a huge range of software, from the humble PowerPoint for presentations to wiki and blog generators, VLEs and private social networks, specialist academic search engines and assessment-preparing packages. Almost all the downloadable software and interactive websites discussed here are free and fairly straightforward to use. Note that web addresses change and that when free software reaches a certain level of complexity it sometimes ceases to be free. Some of the details given here will therefore date fairly quickly. However, it should still give an idea of the range of material available to psychology teachers. When something disappears or ceases to be free you can usually 'Google' an alternative.

PRESENTATION TOOLS

Microsoft PowerPoint is the most commonly used presentation tool in education, industry and just about everywhere. It is also the most commonly used piece of software in the classroom, so it is worthy of a substantial chunk of this chapter. In the 1990s there was great enthusiasm for using PowerPoint as an alternative to the traditional board for delivering information. This is an excellent example of the cyberlemming phenomenon. Teachers soon realised that giving presentations in this way discouraged student activity and interactivity, with the result that the quality of learning visibly declined. There has since been a violent backlash against PowerPoint, criticisms being summed up in the bluntly titled article 'PowerPoint is evil' (Tufte, 2004).

- PowerPoint encourages simplistic thinking by summarising complex ideas on a slide in the form of bullet points or graphs.
- PowerPoint is often used as a cue to remind a teacher of their next point rather than as an aid for the audience.
- PowerPoint encourages teachers to restructure content so that each idea fits on a slide.
- PowerPoint encourages classes to read material only in the order in which it is presented. This can be a disadvantage for students with particular information-processing styles.

How to use PowerPoint badly

PowerPoint looks like a tool for making business presentations – because that's primarily what it is. It was developed by engineers for the purpose of condensing complex technical information for a business audience. Kinchin (2006) uses J.J. Gibson's theory of direct perception to understand why we tend to use it in the same way in education. In the same way that we recognise a chair as a chair because it affords sitting, we recognise PowerPoint as a business presentation tool because it affords listing dense bullet points, and, unless we make a conscious effort to take control, we tend to respond by giving a business pitch rather than a lesson. Figure 7.1 shows a fairly typical PowerPoint slide. There is too much information here, it is all verbal and it is all organised in the form of bullet points.

Something to do with psychology

- First element of the theory in a nice small font to maximise cognitive load
- Second element oversimplified so it fits neatly on one line
- A piece of evidence, just to break up the theory and make it harder to understand
- By now the theory is incomprehensible and quite different from the original
- Third element of the theory – it'll look better with some whizzy animation
- Fourth element. There are five really but I'm running out of space

---

■ **Figure 7.1** A typical PowerPoint slide

Although the unvaried use of bullets is the classic error, adding more visual information will not help if there is too much of it. Consider this slide of the military situation in Afghanistan on the *Guardian*'s datablog: http://www.guardian.co.uk/news/datablog/2010/apr/29/mcchrystal-afghanistan-powerpoint-slide. Confused? Almost certainly. US General McChrystal reportedly said on seeing this slide that 'when we understand that slide we'll have won the war'.

PowerPoint can also be boring. As Cameron (personal communication) points out, if Churchill had had PowerPoint Britain would probably have lost the Second World War. It is hard to inspire with PowerPoint unless we diverge considerably from the business presentation model. One common practice that both adds to boredom and may even make information harder to learn is to read aloud from slides. This prevents us speaking directly to and interacting with our students and, if the information is dense, it may also increase cognitive load because listeners have to simultaneously use auditory and visual channels in short-term memory to process the same information (Maag, 2004).

Cheating death by PowerPoint

As Daniel (2005) says, PowerPoint is just a tool, and examples of its poor use should not put us off attempting to use it properly. From this perspective the current backlash against PowerPoint per se is not really justified. Norvig puts it thus: 'PowerPoint doesn't kill teaching and learning. Teachers and lecturers kill teaching and learning. But using PowerPoint is like having a loaded AK-47 machine-gun on the desk: you can do very unpleasant things with it' (2003:343). There are however a number of ways to avoid doing unpleasant things.

One simple strategy is to use PowerPoint for really short presentations, for example for showing stimulus material at the start of a lesson or topic. This need not even contain words let alone bullet points. Imagery, music and film can interest, inspire and trigger emotional responses from students at least as well as words. It may be that once you get to technical aspects of a theory or study, you decide that PowerPoint is not necessarily the right tool.

If you are going to use PowerPoint for longer and more technical expositions try the following strategies:

■ Use images, not just in the corner of a slide to add variety, but as whole slides to make a point or stimulate discussion. Paivio's dual coding theory predicts that information will be better retained when presented in both visual and verbal form, while theories of learning styles predict that some students will benefit more from visual information and others more from verbal information. Either way students probably benefit from having a good balance of visual and verbal information.

■ Embed or link to video. You can easily find film relevant to many studies, concepts and applications online and download it, for example using Firefox add-ons or file conversion sites like Zamzar (www.zamzar.com). You may find that the film makes your point adequately and you don't need a presentation at all.

■ Put questions, quotes and discussion points on slides as well as information, and make sure you stop talking to give students time to think. PowerPoint affords lecturing but resist the temptation. There is no reason why lessons based around a presentation can't be a much more interactive process.

■ Think really carefully before using bullet points. They are the obvious way to structure a slide and not always wrong, but they are overused. Try boxes and arrows, as in Figure 7.2 to create a more visually interesting slide. You may want to use concept-mapping software (see p118) to generate this sort of display and either use that instead of PowerPoint or export an image of the concept map to put on a slide.

■ Use animation wisely. Too much animation just adds to cognitive load and makes it harder for students to retain the content of a slide, but it is really helpful to be able to call up one packet of information on-screen, explain it, then call up the next rather than presenting a whole slide's worth of information in one hit.

Alternatives to PowerPoint

Although PowerPoint is the best known and most widely used presentation tool there are a variety of alternatives, including some that do essentially the same thing, just slightly differently, and others with quite different purposes and approaches.

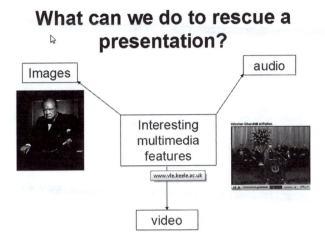

■ **Figure 7.2** A slide with a non-traditional format

Impress (part of Sun Microsystems' Open Office suite)

This is an open source alternative to PowerPoint. The main virtue of Impress is that it is free. This can be important in widening participation; depending on where you teach you may well find that you are limited in your ability to set students homework involving creating presentations by the fact that some students do not have access to PowerPoint at home.[1] In these cases the Open Office suite (http://download.openoffice.org/) is a great alternative. Impress is overall probably as good as PowerPoint, and it has some distinct advantages. For example, it has many of the features of the latest versions of PowerPoint such as exporting a presentation as Flash video – which means you can embed it in a web page – but with a more traditional and user-friendly interface.

Prezi (www.prezi.com)

At the time of writing Prezi is just beginning to make big inroads into the presentation market. It is currently free for educational use when run online, and available as a desktop download at half the commercial price (around £40 a year at time of writing). Prezi takes a brilliantly radical alternative approach to traditional presentation software by replacing slides with a single canvas in which you can zoom in and out (see Figure 7.3). You can pre-set a path for this zooming or spontaneously move around the canvas. Text, links, images and video can be placed on the canvas for zooming. This escapes the rigid sequential information processing encouraged by PowerPoint and Impress. If you like the idea of Prezi but are reluctant to lose your trusty PowerPoint slides there is a solution. In Impress and PowerPoint 2007 you can export the presentation as a Flash video and drop this into your Prezi, although you do lose some animation when you do this.

■ **Figure 7.3**
The Prezi interface

ThinkFree (www.thinkfree.com/)

There are many online presentation tools around. Being online these can be accessed from any computer. ThinkFree is perhaps the most powerful and versatile of these – at least of the free ones – providing the same functions as PowerPoint and Impress. ThinkFree allows you to upload existing PowerPoint files to edit and also to download your presentations in PowerPoint format. Like Impress, ThinkFree is free and so can serve a valuable purpose in widening participation. The interface is very familiar so there is little learning curve for those used to PowerPoint.

VUE (Tufts University)

VUE (which stands for visual understanding environment) is primarily a concept-mapping tool. In terms of both ease of use and features it is arguably the best concept-mapping software. VUE is available free from http://vue.tufts.edu/. A concept map is somewhat like a mind map, but is much more flexible, allowing nodes to be connected in any combination and direction (see Figure 7.4). Nodes can contain text, images and links. VUE also has a presentation mode. This allows you to create a pathway between nodes, rather like in Prezi, and zoom into each node in turn. VUE concept maps can be exported as image files or as web pages.

Powerbullet Presenter

There is currently a move, particularly in high-powered academic conferences, toward using Flash tools to give presentations as opposed to PowerPoint. Flash can be directly embedded in a web page, making it easy to publish, and allows more varied and sophisticated effects to be used than does PowerPoint. Flash presentations can also be embedded into Prezis without losing animation effects – unlike Flash exports from PowerPoint or Impress. Traditionally, Flash tools have been

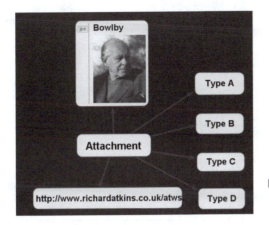

■ **Figure 7.4**
Two nodes from VUE's presentation
mode

expensive and have involved a steep learning curve, hence they have been used by
a small elite group. However, Powerbullet Presenter is free and relatively straightforward to use. It can be downloaded free from http://powerbullet.com/download.
php. Note that, at the time of writing, Mac platforms do not support Flash format.

BEYOND THE POWERPOINT GLASS CEILING

Video and 3-D models as modes of presentation

As we have seen, there are a number of ways of presenting static information
electronically, and this is largely standard practice. However, e-learning specialists sometimes talk about the 'PowerPoint glass ceiling'. What they mean by this
is that many teachers have become confident in the use of presentation software
but do not extend their expertise to other software. By making good use of online
resources including video, 3-D models and experimental simulations we can
considerably extend the quality of students' visual experiences beyond what is
provided by PowerPoint and the like, and provide more opportunities for student-
centred exploration. There are now a number of sites where video of and relevant
to psychology can be found. Some examples are shown in Table 7.1.

Periodically universities make copyright claims and force sites to remove the
videos, hence there will often be dead links on these sites. It is therefore best to
download video when you find it rather than count on it remaining online. There
are also a small number of online 3-D models, particularly useful for studying the
brain. A good example is at www.bbc.so.uk/science/humnanbody/body/interac-
tives/organs/brainmap/index.shtml.

The great advantage of video clips is that they take up very little classroom
time and allow students to visualise things like brain functionality and animal
learning which are inherently interesting but can easily be made dry by too much

■ **Table 7.1** Sources of psychology video material

http://www.youtube.com/	YouTube	video-sharing with loads of psychology
http://www.atpconference.org.uk/ psychotoobies	Psychotoobies	Selected psychology YouTube videos
http://www.learner.org/resources/ series138.html	Discovering psychology	26 30-minute psychology videos
http://freescienceonline.blogspot. com/2007/02/psychology-education- video-and-audio.html	Berkeley University webcasts	video/audio psychology lectures
http://oyc.yale.edu/psychology/ introduction-to-psychology	Yale University webcasts	video/audio psychology lectures
http://www.psychclips.co.uk/	Psychclips	selected psychology video from video-sharing sites

verbal description. In terms of our criteria for effective learning this makes material both more relevant and more memorable. The great thing about 3-D models is that students can explore them at their own pace and construct their own mental representation, meeting the criterion of active learning.

Online simulations and experiments

Also available online are a range of simulations and experiments that can be demonstrated in whole-class teaching via a data projector or performed by students in a computer suite. These also serve the function of bringing psychology to life but have the additional advantage that they involve students in active learning activities. Some examples of online simulations and experiments are shown in Table 7.2. Note that other examples of simulations are provided on p64.

Some of these are metasites and link to several experiments or simulations. Be aware that when sites link to ongoing professional research projects (for example, http://www/socialpsychology.org/expts.him) there is considerable variation in the quality of feedback and debriefing provided to participants. Some topics researched on these sites are somewhat sensitive and may require vetting. Simulations and demonstrations of experiments are usually more straightforward. Be aware as well that some of these sites are much more straightforward to use than others. It is well worth exploring them yourself before letting students loose. As with all online resources, URLs go out of date. Most commonly this is because the institution hosting the material restructures its own website. A good tip to solve a non-functioning link is to go to the institution home page and search from there for what you want.

The use of simulations has attracted the attention of researchers. Venneman and Knowles (2005) evaluated the benefits of Sniffy Lite (Alloway *et al.*, 2000). Sniffy is a virtual rat that can be conditioned to demonstrate various types of

■ **Table 7.2** Some examples of online simulations and experiments

Description	Topic	Current URL
Memory experiments	Eyewitness memory	http://www.youramazingbrain.org.uk/testyourself/eyewitness.htm
	Face recognition	http://psychexps.olemiss.edu/Exps/demoold/aw5demo.htm
	Word recognition	http://psychexps.olemiss.edu/Exps/demoold/aw5demo.htm
Perception and attention experiments	Mental rotation	http://psychexps.olemiss.edu/Exps/demoold/aw5demo.htm
	Various illusions	http://psychexps.olemiss.edu/Exps/demoold/aw5demo.htm
	Dichotic listening	http://psychexps.olemiss.edu/Exps/demoold/aw5demo.htm
Clinical psych simulation	Therapy with ELIZA	http://www.manifestation.com/neurotoys/eliza.php3
Learning simulations	Imprinting	http://samiam.colorado.edu/%7emcclella/expersim/expersim.html
	Classical conditioning	http://www.uwm.edu/~johnchay/cc.htm
	Operant conditioning	http://www.epsych.msstate.edu/adaptive/Fuzz/fuzzapplet.html http://www.uwm.edu/~johnchay/oc2.htm
Social psych experiments	Social facilitation	http://samiam.colorado.edu/%7emcclella/expersim/expersim.html
	Social perceptions	http://www.socialpsychology.org/expts.htm
	Attitudes	http://www.socialpsychology.org/expts.htm
	Implicit associations	http://www.implicit.harvard.edu
Dreaming simulation	EEG, EMG and EOG	http://www.uwm.edu/~johnchay/sl.htm
Personal space simulation	The urinal game	http://flasharcade.com/game.php?urinal
Statistics simulations	Graphs simulations	http://www.kuleuven.ac.be/ucs/java/ http://www.shodor.org/interactivate/activities/index.html
	Correlation and regression simulations	http://noppa5.pc.helsinki.fi/koe/corr/index.html http://www.martindalecenter.com/
	Numerous stats simulations	http://www.ruf.rice.edu/~lane/stat_sim/index.html

learning. The Lite version is simpler and Sniffy just undergoes classical and operant conditioning. In an experimental procedure Venneman and Knowles found that American psychology undergraduates using Sniffy outperformed a control group and rated Sniffy highly. Although versatile and reasonably good value (around £15 per machine), I found Sniffy to be lacking in user-friendliness and much preferred the simpler free online conditioning simulations shown in Table 7.2.

Web-cams

Teaching observational research can now involve practical exercises without students having to leave their seats. There are numerous online web-cams the output of which can be accessed over the Internet – be a little cautious if you carry out a search for these as many hits will link to adult sites. There are important ethical and legal issues to consider here. Under the Data Protection Act it is illegal to use surveillance techniques for anything other than security purposes and to do anything with that data other than keep it for a limited period and then destroy it, unless everyone that might be observed has given full permission (see also p64). This means that although it is quite possible to access web-cams in public places online, it is not ethical. Even the observation of controlled situations like the *Big Brother* house, where observees will have given full permission and are aware they are being watched, raise some thorny issues. What is possible and ethically acceptable however is to use web-cams in zoos to observe animal behaviour. Table 7.3 shows the URLs of some zoos that have live online web-cam feeds.

One tip for using zoo web-cams is to bear in mind that they are frequently offline. Make sure that you have a few options lined up before starting a lesson.

THE INTERNET AS A SEARCH TOOL

As we have already seen the Internet provides a wealth of resources for the psychology teacher, ranging from video, simulations, experiments, statistical analysis and web-cams. You might think it odd, but one of the harder things to do using the Net can be to find good quality information. As a source of information about psychology the Net has great potential but can be very frustrating. On one hand, web browsers such as Firefox and Opera have provided an unprecedented opportunity for students to explore the world, asking their own questions and seeking their own sources of information (Churach and Fisher, 2001). On the other hand, unless you set tasks up carefully, most exploration using the Net tends to be quite superficial (Sellinger, 2001), students simply locating and re-presenting pre-existing

■ **Table 7.3** Some examples of zoos with live web-cam feeds

Zoo	Observable animals	Current URL
Smithsonian Zoo	Ferrets, tigers, mole-rats, kingfishers, giraffes, pandas, octopus	http://nationalzoo.si.edu/Animals/WebCams/
Melbourne Zoo	Gorillas, butterflies	http://www.zoo.org.au/featured/webcams.cfm
San Diego Zoo	Polar bears, pandas, apes, elephants	http://sandiegozoo.org/videos/
Welsh Mountain Zoo	African birds	http://www.welshmountainzoo.org/camstream.htm

materials rather than making the decisions and following lines of enquiry that would make searching a constructive task.

The place of searching in the modern curriculum

Like practical work, the role of Internet searching has become less obvious with recent curriculum overhauls. Like the move away from practical work this change carries with it the risk that transferable skills traditionally associated with studying psychology are being lost. Pre-2000, when exams were primarily essay-based, students could put together their own notes, reasonably safe in the knowledge that anything relevant they found could be used in an exam. With the advent of short-answer questions and more closely prescribed specification content this has become a much more dicey strategy. Internet searching also had a place in working up coursework but, of course, this has been lost. Thinking strategically, there is little pragmatic reason why psychology students undertaking the current curricula should ever search for material. Or is there? I would suggest that there are strategic as well as more holistic reasons for keeping an element of searching in psychology teaching:

- *Deep processing leads to better retention of information.* As long as searching is in the context of a task that captures student interest – such as a problem-based learning task – see p41 – students engaged in searches are likely to process what they find deeply and so remember it well. Introducing a meta-cognitive element to searching – as in webquesting, see p124 – has been demonstrated to further enhance retention.
- *Searching facilitates differentiation.* By offering open-ended tasks and explicit choices in search tasks it is possible for students to select different levels of sophistication in the information they seek out. This can be very effective in differentiation, as some students use the task to consolidate their understanding of the basics and others to extend their knowledge.
- *Properly constructed search tasks make interesting homework.* Although searching can be inconvenient in the classroom because of the time and ICT requirements, it has some significant advantages as an independent study task. Students have the necessary equipment and searching requires less self-discipline than practice exam questions at the end of a long tiring day. Also, students who skimp on or fail to complete this sort of homework are not jeopardising their attainment, unlike those who fail to get down to exam-based homework.

To Google and beyond: search engines and databases

The obvious Internet task that most of us start out by setting is very general in nature and uses a conventional search engine. However, this approach often results in the following problems:

■ There are a huge number of hits and it is unclear which ones to follow up. Often the first few pages of hits are there because the site owners have paid developers to get them there. They are not necessarily the most useful sites.

■ Typically, each site has a small volume of information that rarely goes beyond what is in student textbooks.

■ Many sites are of very dubious quality, containing incorrect information or with a 'pop-psychology' focus.

■ Many sites are actually metasites, most links from which simply connect to each other, leaving the searcher going around in circles.

■ Just as the search looks like it is getting somewhere it becomes apparent that the searcher either needs access codes or a credit card to get to the worthwhile information.

This is not to diss Google and the like. Modern search engines are technologically amazing, but they can only work with the sites on the Internet and the search terms students input. Universities subscribe to a range of specialist online databases containing articles from journals. Schools and colleges cannot afford to do this, and much of the material would not be appropriate anyway. There is, however, a good range of differentiated search tools around that can be accessed free. The most basic tools are psychology dictionaries and encyclopedias, the most advanced repositories of full-text articles. Examples are shown in Table 7.4.

The British Library (http://direct.bl.uk/bld.Home.do) will provide full text of any article within a day or two for a small fee. One of the great advantages of using databases and specialist search engines is that they require students to actively make decisions about what key words to search for, what hits to follow up, what to print out, etc. Students working together can take decisions jointly. Thus this type of searching can be an authentic constructivist activity (see p40 for a discussion).

Webquesting: an answer to the 'how' of searching

One approach to structuring search tasks is the webquest (Dodge, 1995). Webquests aim to provide the kind of information students need to carry out a search alongside a metacognitive framework for making sure they get the most out of the experience and process information deeply. A typical webquest has the following elements:

■ An introduction to the topic and the aim of tasks.

■ The task, which is typically enquiry or problem-based (see p41). This may include a breakdown of stages and roles for group members.

■ Resources, a list of websites or search tools recommended for the task.

■ Reflection on the task, perhaps including a summary of what has been learned and an evaluation of its usefulness.

A webquest generator can be found at http://www.aula21.net/Wqfacil/webeng.htm. However it is straightforward to construct a web page yourself that

■ **Table 7.4** Examples of free online databases and specialist search engines, differentiated by level

Title	Description	Current URL	Level
AllPsych	Psychology dictionary	http://allpsych.com/dictionary.html	Simple
ITS	Psychology dictionary	http://www.tuition.com.hk/psychology/	
Dictionary of Psychology	Psychology dictionary	http://dictionary-psychology.com/	
Alleydog	Psychology encyclopedia	http://www.alleydog.com/	
JRank	Psychology encyclopedia	http://psychology.jrank.org/	
Encyclopaedia of Psychology	Psychology portal	http://www.psychology.org/	
The Psychologist archive	Back issues of *The Psychologist* magazine	http://www.thepsychologist.org.uk/archive/archive_home.cfm	
PubMed	Database of abstracts	http://www.pubmed.gov	
Ingenta	Database of abstracts	http://www.ingentaconnect.com/	
Google Scholar	Specialist search engine	http://scholar.google.com/	
PsychCrawler	Specialist search engine	http://www.psychcrawler.com/	
Scirus	Specialist search engine	http://www.scirus.com/srsapp/	
PsychClassics	Repository of full text articles	http://psychclassics.yorku.ca/	Complex

includes the necessary elements. If your school or college has a VLE this will have a web-page builder function.

VIRTUAL LEARNING ENVIRONMENTS

Ofsted have defined a virtual learning environment (or VLE) as 'a computer-based system that helps learning' (2009: 8). This is a deliberately broad term used to avoid bias between the different ways of and tools for organising learning materials online. In a managerial sense then any website on which learning materials are organised can be called a virtual learning environment. More technically speaking, a VLE is a particular sort of website or content management system adapted to education in the following ways:

■   A VLE is structured in such a way that material is organised into courses, and within courses into logical divisions like topics or weeks.
■   Students can register on a VLE and access their course or courses.

- A VLE has education-specific tools, for example for building quizzes, submitting assignments and recording marks.
- A VLE has various levels of access so that teachers can create courses and materials while students can just see resources and complete tasks.

One of the aims when VLE technology was developed was to reduce costs by reducing teacher input. This has largely failed to materialise – so far anyway – and VLEs are more likely at present to be used for supporting rather than replacing conventional courses. There are a number of VLE systems around. Some, like Blackboard, WebCT and Frog are commercial. Others like Moodle are free and open source. Several studies (for example, Suri and Schuhmacher, 2008) have concluded that pedagogically Moodle is the best system, although other factors such as ease of linking up to the school or college management information system also play a part in the choice of system.

If your school or college does not have a VLE, or you dislike it, it is actually surprisingly straightforward to host your own, although it is worth checking whether your management will see this move as innovation or subversion! Many web-hosting companies (for example, Wiser Hosting, www.wiserhosting.co.uk) include access to c-panel, which can auto-install Moodle. You do not need any other website infrastructure if you do not want it, just your Moodle, which is installed more or less at the touch of a button. See http://moodle.org/ for instructions on setting up courses and registering students in Moodle.

Structuring and resourcing a VLE

This could easily be a whole book in itself, so what follows is really a potted version of the topic. A VLE can be used in different ways. If you get a choice, structure courses by topic rather than by week. Weekly layouts often appeal to managers because they make you look well organised and elaborately planned. However, you only have to have one unplanned absence or a trip arranged after the VLE is constructed to throw your weekly plan out and confuse students about where they should be for weeks or months. Topic-formats are much more flexible. Under each topic you have the opportunity to add static resources such as documents, presentations and links, and more interactive ones such as quizzes, assessments and, depending on the system, forums, chat-rooms, wikis, etc. An example is shown in Figure 7.5.

One way of making a VLE more user-friendly than the traditional vertical column of resources is to use learning hubs. A learning hub takes the resources for a topic or subtopic and weaves them into a narrative, with each resource hyperlinked from the text. The narrative serves as a summary of the topic. An example is shown in Figure 7.6.

Now you have to give thought to how you will use the VLE. Teachers who have assumed their students will spontaneously flock to it in their spare time have often been sadly disappointed. If you want students to interact regularly and productively with the VLE you have to have some interactive content, both in the form of quizzes and assignments but perhaps also some Web 2.0 applications such as forums and wikis. It is also helpful to make the course front page more dynamic by adding RSS feeds – this is easy in Moodle, harder in some other systems. RSS feeds can connect, for example, to psychology news sites (see p101 for a list), so that when students log on they can see stories both of news from within psychology and of psychology being applied to explaining the general news. Once these feeds are set up the content will change regularly without maintenance. Figure 7.7 shows a feed from the British Psychological Society's Research Digest in Moodle.

Interactive and dynamic content will make your VLE more appealing to students, but you still need to consider how to use it. One useful strategy is to use your learning hubs or topic resource-lists to order lessons, for example, show a video, give a presentation, followed by a quiz. Having a webquest or practice exam question to follow up the lesson in homework then appears more natural. Of course there is a steep investment of time required to populate a course with all these resources, but once it is done properly that's the basics of your preparation done until the next specification revision, leaving you free to be more creative with fine-tuning your personalisation etc.

Tools for creating online questions

There are a range of existing quizzes to be found on the Internet. Some sources are shown in Table 7.5. You can also download good and free software called HotPotatoes to make your own quizzes from here: http://hotpot.uvic.ca/. Your VLE will probably have some tools for quiz creation but these are permanently part of your VLE – you cannot extract your quizzes and take them with you when you change jobs unless they are built with separate software. On the other hand, it is not straightforward to automatically record student results from HotPotatoes quizzes.

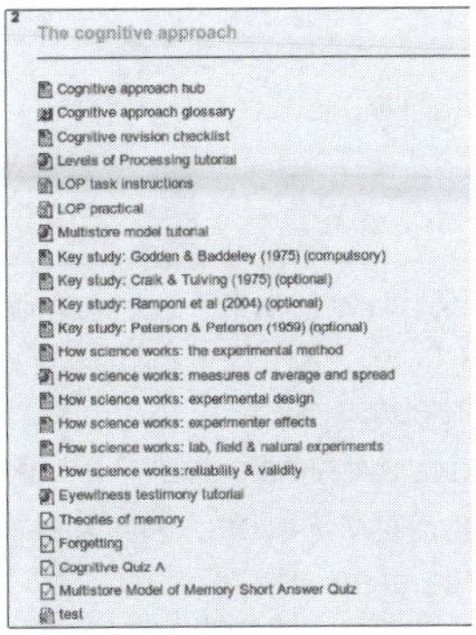

Figure 7.5 Resources for a topic in Moodle

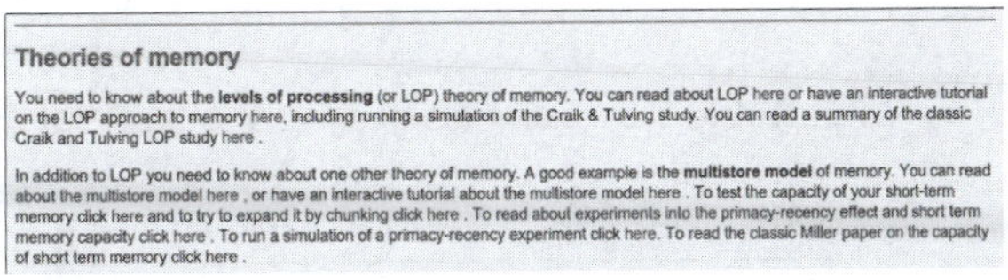

Figure 7.6 A section from a learning hub

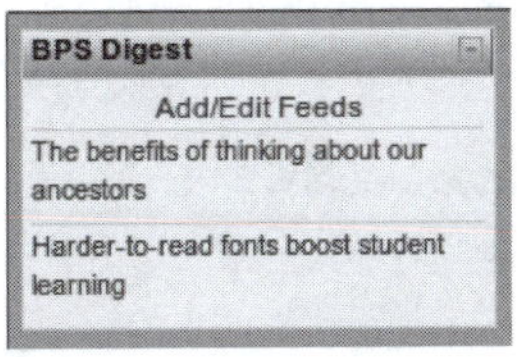

Figure 7.7 A news feed from the BPS Research Digest in Moodle

The best quiz-building tools are those that meet SCORM standards. These will generate quiz files that are both portable from one VLE to another and fully integrate into the VLE so that results can be easily recorded. Examples of free SCORM generators are Exe (http://exelearning.org/wiki) and Courselab (http://www.courselab.com/). There is a slightly steeper learning curve to use these than HotPotatoes or built-in VLE tools.

Effectiveness of VLEs

Bolam (2004) makes an impressive case for the benefits of adopting an e-learning approach in a post-16 psychology department. He describes a model used in an independent girls' school in Jersey. This involved course materials being made available by e-learning, with conventional back-up of one lecture a week, one 'normal' lesson and a small-group tutorial. The benefits of this are described as follows:

■ Students are accountable for their own learning.
■ Small groups allow meaningful discussion.
■ Free time is created so that marking can be completed in the working day.
■ There is more time to give feedback to students.
■ There is quicker and better development of the student–teacher relationship.
■ Students complete more written work.
■ There is more time to focus on skills as well as content.
■ Gaps in understanding are quickly identified.
■ Differentiation is easier to achieve because of the small group sessions.

Some studies have compared outcomes in psychology classes using VLE-based and traditional delivery. Mottarella *et al.* (2005) describe an experiment in which American psychology undergraduates took introductory modules in basic learning theory in one of three conditions: traditional classroom, web-enhanced and

■ **Table 7.5** Examples of sites with online question banks

Title	Owners/developers	Current URL
PsychExchange	Mark Holah & Jamie Davies	http://www.psychexchange.co.uk/
Psyweb	Nelson Thornes	http://www.nelsonthornes.com/courses/psyweb/
Psyonline	A consortium of schools	http://psyonline.edgehill.ac.uk/
Psychology Together	Psychology Together	http://www.Psychologytogether.com
Gerard Keegan	Gerry Keegan	http://www.gerardkeegan.co.uk
Psychlotron	Psychlotron	http://www.psychology.pwp.blueyonder.co.uk/

entirely web-based. Those in the web-based condition did significantly worse than the other two groups. Other studies have found mixed results. Maki *et al.* (2000) compared exam grades and student satisfaction in an introductory psychology course taught by lectures or by interactive web-based software. The web-based condition was associated with better exam results but poorer student satisfaction. These findings illustrate the risks of embracing e-learning without elaborate and well thought-out support, as was provided in the Bolam case study.

WEB 2.0: MAXIMISING STUDENT INVOLVEMENT

VLE technology has never become ubiquitous, and teachers and institutions vary enormously in the emphasis they place on using this kind of technology. However, some commentators are saying that the VLE concept is already obsolete due to the growth of Web 2.0 technology. The term 'Web 2.0' has been around since around 2004–5 – there is a geeky debate about who said it first if you are interested. Web 2.0 is defined by McLoughlin and Lee (2007) as 'a second generation, or more personalised, communicative form of the World Wide Web that emphasises active participation, connectivity, collaboration and sharing of knowledge and ideas among users' (2007: 665). Some examples of Web 2.0 applications are defined in Table 7.6.

VLEs and Web 2.0: is it an either/or thing?

We are currently teaching the first generation of true 'digital natives', young people who have never known a time without ICT, and it is important to understand how they use technology. The problem with VLE technology as it is most obviously used is that it is a top-down process with teachers providing static resources for students to passively download and use. As Sheely says: 'we can't stop lecturing online' (2006; cited in McLoughlin and Lee, 2007: 668). But this is not how young people use the Internet. Outside education, students spend time social-networking,

■ **Table 7.6** Some Web 2.0 terms defined

Term	Definition
Wiki	A website where users can be given rights to add their own content
Blog	A website where content appears in particular order, most recent first
Forum	A space designed for discussion between members
Social network	A web-based community of individuals who can monitor each other's web space and communicate with one another
RSS	A system for feeding information from one website to another so that when one is updated so is the other
Social bookmarking	A system for flagging up online content for other users to see

blogging, contributing to as well as taking from wikis, subscribing to RSS feeds, file-sharing and social-bookmarking. Note the number of verbs in this sentence; these ways of using the Internet are highly active and interactive processes in which students make and act on decisions rather than being passively led.

The situation with VLEs is much like that with PowerPoint. In the same way as PowerPoint looks like a tool for giving bulleted business presentations, a VLE looks like a tool for placing static resources online for students to read. Once you are aware of that it becomes your choice how you use it. Some VLEs, notably Moodle, have Web 2.0 functionality, so you can add a wiki as easily as a handout. We just tend not to because we can see much more easily the logical link between a handout and the summative exam than that between a wiki and the same exam. A good tip is to put a relatively small number of handouts and presentations on your VLE so that they do not outnumber the interactive features and make the course page appear top-down and passive.

Although some VLEs have some Web 2.0 functionality, it is worth bearing in mind that there are numerous free online resources that are purpose-made for Web 2.0 development. These are typically more attractive than VLE forums or wiki functions and are more congruent with the type of sites students use outside education. One tip is to maintain some of these separate from your VLE and link from it. While some e-learning experts see VLEs and Web 2.0 as rival technology and fiercely take the side of one or other, there is no reason why they should not be used together.

Practical uses of Web 2.0 in the psychology classroom

There is no doubt that students use Web 2.0 for informal learning (Selwyn, 2007). However, this is not the same as saying that Web 2.0 necessarily lends itself to classroom use, and you can be forgiven for wondering just what to do with a wiki or forum, particularly if you don't use these things yourself. The following are just some simple suggestions based on things I have tried or seen.

Application of psychology to real life

This can be done using blog or forum technology. Cut and paste or link to a news story and ask students to explain, collectively, in groups or individually, how psychology could be used to explain the event. The rule is that each group or individual must add something. This is not a particularly arduous task but it forces students to engage with the material. The advantage of having this on a forum or blog over paper is that students can learn from each other's ideas and internalise the skills of application.

AO2 elaboration

This can be done using a blog or wiki. Provide a stimulus study, theory or application and a basic cut-down evaluation. Ask students to each produce an expanded version. They can look at each other's ideas but their wording must be their own. One thing that limits students' ability to provide detailed evaluation is the lack of suitable examples. The elaboration task allows students to engage with AO2 with plenty of suitable material to work from.

Peer marking

One way to teach students how to use awarding body mark-schemes is to place examples on a blog or wiki and have students peer-mark them, then argue for their choice of mark. The advantage of doing this in a Web 2.0 environment is the ability to follow each other's logic and actively construct one's own view.

Research design

This lends itself to blog, forum or wiki. Set students a design task, for example, 'How would you go about investigating the following research question?' In groups students come up with a design. Each group member has to contribute a design feature, so you might want to provide a list of features for students to work from. Each group then critiques the other groups' designs, developing both AO2 and AO3 skills.

Class-generated notes

This one works best with wiki technology, and it requires that you either have strong nerves or are prepared to intervene, because it involves students taking on a lot of responsibility. Give a class a small section of the specification and have them put together their own resources. You will need to cue them in with the specification content and some likely sources of information.

Pooled revision notes

Students revise in different ways, and there is never enough time for them to try all strategies. One way around this is to have students pool their flash cards, mind-maps, concept maps and MP3-format notes via a Web 2.0 environment. Wikis or private social networks probably work best for this.

Recommended Web 2.0 tools and sites

Table 7.7 shows some examples of Web 2.0 tools that are either entirely free or offer decent free packages. These are just recommendations – you may well find

■ **Table 7.7** Examples of free and user-friendly Web 2.0 tools

Blogging tools	WordPress	http://wordpress.com/
	Blogger	https://www.blogger.com/start
Wiki builder	WetPaint	www.wetpaint.com/
	Wikia	www.wikia.com/Wikia
Private social network builder	Spruz	www.spruz.com/
Forums	MakeForum	http://www.makeforum.org/
	Lefora	http://www.lefora.com/
Social bookmarking	Digg	http://digg.com/
	Delicious	http://delicious.com/
	Stumbleupon	http://www.stumbleupon.com/

your own sites that you prefer. Also remember that URLs change and free resources sometimes cease to be free.

CONCLUSIONS AND REFLECTIONS

Following some notable early failures and false starts, e-learning is now firmly established as an important part of education, and we are at the point where a good range of software and online resources is available. However, some of the key educational tools, in particular presentation packages and VLEs, are probably best used in non-obvious ways, so it is critical to keep in mind how students learn and the place of technology in the lives of the first digital native generation. Depending on what you want to achieve alternatives to the standard tools may do a better job, so have a look at Prezi and WetPaint as well as PowerPoint and Moodle.

Bear in mind though that ICT is always just a tool, never an end in itself. If a particular application that is being pushed by your management does not fit with your teaching style or philosophy, that happens to the geekiest of us sometimes, and it certainly does not make you a bad person or a bad teacher. ICT is extremely diverse, and we all have our preferred applications. No one likes or works well with all ICT tools – you will notice that I have not even mentioned interactive whiteboards in this chapter. I do believe though that somewhere there is a website or a piece of software for everyone that, used right, can enhance their teaching.

QUESTIONS FOR REFLECTION

1   Do you use as much ICT as you would like or think you should? If not what are the barriers to using it more?
2   How do you feel about your PowerPoint presentations after reading this chapter?
3   Have you broken the PowerPoint glass ceiling?
4   Do you use search tasks? How can you reconcile these with the current crowded and prescriptive curriculum?

5　Does your school or college make good use of a VLE? How do you find it and how might you improve it?

6　Has Web 2.0 reached your classroom yet? What plans do you have in this direction?

NOTE

1　For students wishing to view your presentations at home Microsoft does supply a free PowerPoint viewer.

FURTHER READING

Bolam, P. (2004) A case study on the development and use of an e-learning initiative. *Psychology Teaching* **Summer**, 39–45.

JISC (2008) *Exploring tangible benefits of e-learning*. Northumbria University.

Ofsted (2009) *Virtual learning environment: an evaluation of their development in a sample of educational settings*. London, Ofsted.

MEETING THE DIVERSE NEEDS OF PSYCHOLOGY STUDENTS

By the end of this chapter you should be able to:

■ Appreciate the range of social and psychological variables impacting on student experience and success.
■ Understand the range of cognitive variables affecting student performance, and offer a contemporary definition of differentiation.
■ Discuss the possible relationships between intelligence, ability and achievement, and apply a range of strategies to help students of varying ability.
■ Explain the importance of learning style and learning strategies in affecting achievement, and offer approaches to working with students of differing style and strategy.
■ Understand the additional challenge faced by dyslexic students and be aware of some ways in which ICT can be used to support them.
■ Outline factors affecting motivation, including self-efficacy and attributions, and suggest strategies to enhance motivation.
■ Identify gender issues in the psychology curriculum, resources and classroom, and discuss how gender can impact on achievement.

Like virtually any group of people, psychology students are extremely diverse and so have differing needs. Pause for a moment and think about just how many variables may impact on a student's experience of studying psychology. Aside from demographic factors such as age, gender, socio-economic status, ethnicity, culture and subculture, religion, sexual orientation and disability, we also need to think about the importance of individual cognitive differences, for example in intelligence, information-processing (learning) style, learning strategy and motivation. Thinking about consciously catering for all these variables all the time is likely to bring on cognitive overload.

However, catering for diversity is fundamental to teaching. If you have come to education from a business background, your experience may be that diversity issues are peripheral to the company mission, considered to satisfy legal requirements for equality of opportunity, probably as an afterthought, perhaps even an inconvenience. In teaching, diversity is absolutely central. No one pays us to teach some of our students. This is not to trivialise the challenge of meeting diverse student needs, but if we are not at least trying in good faith to cater to all our students we are not doing our job at all. Although this is a challenging idea it should actually sit pretty comfortably with psychology teachers. After all, as Ocampo *et al.* (2003) say, we are working with psychology, a discipline devoted to improving quality of life. We should therefore embrace efforts to improve the experience of studying for all. For teachers, there is little doubt that this brings additional challenges but also rewards.

DEFINING DIFFERENTIATION FOR THE 21ST CENTURY

Although the concept of differentiation has been around for a while, its meaning has changed over time. The traditional definition involves providing alternative resources and activities for students of differing ability. While doing this may form a part of a differentiation strategy, more modern and sophisticated views of differentiation depart from tradition in two ways. First differentiation is now widely seen as being according to student need rather than ability. Ability may be one of the variables taken into account in differentiating, but other factors such as learning style, learning strategy, learning difficulty, motivation and gender can be equally important. Second, differentiation need not mean providing separate tasks and resources for different groups, just that the range of tasks and resources we use is suitable for a range of students.

So how do we take account of these variables? For quality assurance purposes there are no prescribed differentiation strategies, although Ofsted requires evidence that teachers are aware of individual differences in student needs and that assessments are used to inform individuals of their progress. With the current emphasis on making the most of limited time, for practical purposes extension activities are pretty much a requirement. BECTA (2003) suggest four strands to differentiation:

- *Differentiation by resource*: using resources that are accessible to a range of students.
- *Differentiation by task*: setting tasks that are suitable for a range of students.
- *Differentiation by support*: providing support mechanisms suitable for a range of students.
- *Differentiation by response*: providing feedback that identifies student characteristics and suggests ways forward.

These four strands of differentiation run through this chapter.

ABILITY AND INTELLIGENCE

It is a truism that students vary in their ability to successfully negotiate the sort of assessments made in post-16 psychology. Common sense suggests that one factor impacting on this ability to perform in psychology is intelligence – in fact as teachers we are often guilty of confusing ability and intelligence. Psychology teachers, however, should know better than to trust common sense – actually there is a surprisingly small body of evidence to suggest that intelligence – at least as measured by IQ tests – is related to achievement in psychology, and even this needs unpicking further before the true relationships are revealed. In one recent study Diseth (2002) assessed 89 Norwegian psychology students for IQ using the Wechsler scale (WAIS). Only the vocabulary sub-scale of verbal intelligence predicted achievement in psychology exams. This relationship is perhaps not surprising – psychology is a language all of its own so we would expect success to be linked to vocabulary. The Diseth study is particularly important in demonstrating that intelligence and success in psychology are not synonymous or even necessarily related.

It pays to be equally wary of the idea of academic ability. Intelligence is a controversial idea for many reasons but it can at least be precisely defined and reliably measured. Ability on the other hand is simply a pragmatic term used to describe our impressions of how our students are doing, what we think they might be capable of or some awkward hybrid of these two (Jarvis, 2005). We might use prior achievement to try to define ability more objectively, but correlations between achievement at one educational level and the next are more modest than you might think. In one study, for example, Jarvis (2006a) found correlations of around +0.5 between combined GCSE score and AS-level marks in psychology. Value-added systems that define a student's 'potential' by their prior achievement are a logical nonsense, as well as displaying monstrous arrogance in presuming to understand human potential as a set of GCSE results. All A-level teachers will be able to recall students who came to psychology with the minimum required GCSEs but who blossomed academically out of all recognition when they came to know psychology. Because of this we should avoid labelling students with a fixed ability.

Taking out notions of intelligence and ability, it is still important to use teaching strategies that are appropriate for students with a range of current success in our classes. This need not involve rethinking all the ways you teach, just being aware of their significance. Consider the ideas discussed in this book. Co-operative learning and peer tutoring allow students of currently 'low ability' to pick up skills from peers. Problem-based learning tasks and references to popular culture allow students unused to or uncomfortable with thinking in abstract terms to concretise psychological concepts. When we teach psychological thinking we are not merely drilling students for AO2 questions, but actually developing the skills needed to take their thinking to another level. By considering textual variables we can construct student resources that are no less conceptually advanced but far more accessible to students with a range of reading ability. When we use ICT we are shifting away from the traditional classroom with its historical connotations of class distinction towards a more modern and egalitarian system. Box 8.1 summarises strategies to help cater to a range of current ability.

Implicit theories of intelligence

One theme emerging from the last section is that talking in terms of student ability and linking this to intelligence causes problems because, in the Western world, we have a tendency to see these variables as unchangeable. This is in contrast to attitudes in other cultures where intelligence is closely linked to effort and motivation. It may be then that, when it comes to understanding student achievement, intelligence per se is less important than what students believe about intelligence. We owe much of our understanding of this implicit theory of intelligence phenomenon to the American psychologist Carol Dweck and her colleagues, who distinguish between entity and incremental theories. Entity theorists see intelligence as fixed whereas incremental theorists see it as changeable. Bandura and Dweck (1981) noted that their students were preoccupied with their intelligence and speculated that this appeared to be related to the their belief that intelligence was a fixed quantity. The idea that we have a limited quantity of intelligence and that it may or may not be enough to achieve our goals naturally makes students anxious and can be demotivating. If we share this idea then we are unlikely to encourage students currently not achieving highly to do so. Dweck *et al.* (1995) developed a tool for measuring students' implicit beliefs about intelligence. The Implicit Theories of Intelligence Scale is shown in Box 8.2.

■ **Box 8.1 Strategies to differentiate by ability**

■ Focus on developing skills. Much of the disparity between 'high ability' and 'low ability' students is not something invariant but simply their mastery of cognitive and metacognitive skills such as question analysis, planning and critical thinking. These can all be taught.

■ The wider the range of current ability in a teaching group the more time should be spent in student-centred activities that allow students to work at their own pace.

■ Consider using group work in which currently high and low achieving students are put together and consider implementing a programme of peer tutoring.

■ Experiment with manipulating text variables and pedagogical features and see whether resources can be made more user-friendly without compromising their rigour.

■ Make reference to popular culture. This helps link what can be very abstract principles to the everyday experience of students.

■ Use more ICT. There is emerging evidence that ICT serves as a leveller between students of differing socio-economic status.

■ Visibly adopt the attitude that ability is not fixed but changeable. There is a body of research showing that student motivation can be manipulated in this way.

■ **Box 8.2 The Implicit Theories of Intelligence Scale (adult version)** (Reproduced from Dweck, 2000)

Read each sentence below and circle the one number that shows how much you agree with it. There are no right or wrong answers.

1	2	3	4	5	6
Strongly agree	Agree	Mostly agree	Mostly disagree	Disagree	Strongly disagree

___ 1 You have a certain amount of intelligence and you can't do much to change it.
___ 2 Your intelligence is something about you that you can't change very much.
___ 3 No matter who you are you can change your intelligence a lot.
___ 4 To be honest, you can't really change how intelligent you are.
___ 5 You can always substantially change how intelligent you are.
___ 6 You can learn new things, but you can't really change your basic intelligence.
___ 7 No matter how much intelligence you have you can always change it quite a bit.
___ 8 You can change even your basic intelligence level considerably.

To obtain a score, add up the numbers from questions 1, 2, 4 and 6, and the reverse scores from 3, 5, 7 and 8. You will have a score between 8 and 48. The higher your score the more of an incremental theory you have.

Studies have consistently shown that incremental beliefs are associated with high achievement (see for example Faria, 1998), and even that they can be more predictive of student achievement than IQ. Studies have also shown that students from lower socio-economic groups are more likely to adopt an entity theory (Faria and Fontaine, 1997). This points towards a practical application in improving the motivation of working class students. It is perhaps even more important to see academic ability as changeable. If IQ is to some extent modifiable, academic ability is surely more so – developing higher-level thinking skills (Chapter 5) and revision strategies (Chapter 3) can transform students' ability to achieve in post-16 psychology beyond recognition. It is important though that psychology teachers adopt an incremental position – if we do not believe we can transform academic ability then there is little incentive to work with student skills.

Dweck's work has further implications for challenging student stereotypes. Levy *et al.* (1998) gave college students an article (fictitious) that made a strong case for either entity theory or incremental theory. The students then undertook an apparently unrelated task of assessing the accuracy of stereotypes of ethnic and occupational groups. Those who had read the entity theory article concurred with the stereotypes to a much greater extent than those who had studied the incremental article. This and related studies suggest that successful challenging of entity beliefs in students can have a direct impact on their social development.

LEARNING STYLES AND STRATEGIES

The past two decades have seen a growing appreciation of the fact that students vary not just quantitatively as a function of their ability – however we conceive of that – but also qualitatively according to the ways in which they process information and orient towards different subject matter, teaching style, study habits and mode of information presentation. For example, following on from the Piagetian tradition, teachers have tended to see orientation towards concrete rather than abstract ideas as cognitive immaturity or low intelligence. A more modern and less pejorative interpretation is that a student with a strong preference for concrete ideas is demonstrating a particular information-processing style. Table 8.1 shows some scenarios in which learning style might affect the study of psychology.

Looking at the scenarios shown in Table 8.1 the explanatory power of the learning styles construct is clear. However, two major problems facing those working with learning styles also leap out. First, to explain different scenarios we need a number of classifications of learning styles. In the broadest sense of the term, all qualitative variations in learning can be thought of as learning styles, but this lack of precise definition is also a problem because it means that there is little agreement about what learning styles actually are (Reynolds, 1997). In their classic

■ **Table 8.1** Using learning styles to explain common problems

Scenario	Possible learning styles interpretation	Classification system
Jo has difficulty making sense of extended prose. When she sees psychology in diagrammatic form however it presents no problems.	Jo has a visual rather than a verbal learning style.	Riding (1991) Felder and Silverman (1986)
Will has no problem understanding psychological studies but has difficulty with more abstract theoretical ideas.	Will has a concrete rather than abstract learning style.	Gregorc (1979)
Amy gets on well with exam questions that are based on real-life scenarios or which have a lead-in quote but finds questions on their own out of a context confusing.	Amy is highly field-dependent, and is disadvantaged in the exam system as against more field-independent students.	Witkin (1964)
John studies straight sciences. In psychology he enjoys research methods, biopsychology and learning theory. He is however stumped by Freudian theory and social constructionism.	John has an analytic or sequential learning style, as opposed to a global or wholist style, and copes with logical progressions of ideas better than 'big picture' issues.	Riding (1991) Felder and Silverman (1986)

review Coffield *et al.* (2004) identified 71 distinct learning styles classifications, of which 13 could be classified as 'major models' based on their theoretical importance, widespread use and influence on the development of later models. A second problem is that although we can interpret the problems these students are having by means of a particular learning style, it is hard to know whether this is the correct interpretation. The theoretical basis of learning styles is thus very weak, although they undoubtedly exist.

There are additional problems with the learning styles construct. We cannot currently measure learning styles in a reliable or valid way; the psychometric properties of learning style instruments vary widely and they usually fail to meet the standards of reliability and validity attained by standard IQ and personality trait inventories. In addition – forget the grand claims made by commercial dealers of learning styles packages – there is no consensus among researchers about the best way to respond to student learning styles. Typically, teachers receive feedback about each student and recommendations for how best to cater to their needs. This makes the assumption that student learning can be enhanced when a teacher modifies their style to fit more closely with the learning style of their students. However there is no clear evidence that this is helpful for the student (Pheiffer *et al.*, 2003).

Applications of learning styles research

Much of the research and practice currently carried out based on learning styles is probably little more than pop psychology. So has anything useful come from learning styles research? Actually I would suggest that, yes, there are three potential benefits to thinking in terms of learning style. First, the idea of learning styles encourages teachers to think about students in terms of meeting their differing needs as opposed to labelling their ability. Second, it encourages teachers to employ a variety of teaching and assessment methods in order to cater for students with different (for lack of a better term) learning styles – this variety is almost certainly beneficial. For example, we can easily make use of pictures, diagrams and graphs to encourage visual processing (the visual–verbal distinction is probably a sound one – see Riding and Rayner, 1998).

Finally, there are instances in classroom teaching when learning styles research can inform our feedback to students to their benefit. For example, there is research suggesting that psychology students with a visual – as opposed to verbal – learning style particularly benefit from the use of ICT in lessons (Smith and Woody, 2000). We can respond to a student who is aware that they have a strongly visual learning style – or indeed one who appears to be thrown by extended text – by suggesting that they make more use of ICT in their study, particularly using software like VUE (p118) that structures information in a highly visual form.

Research also shows that students with a sequential as opposed to global learning style often orient to science subjects and are thus more likely to be comfortable with the hard science aspects of psychology. It can be helpful to spot this and work to prevent disenchantment with psychology, suggesting to the student something along the lines of: 'You don't like Freud much. You do sciences don't you? Hang in there, most of the course is more scientific than this.' No explicit reference to learning styles is needed for this type of intervention, merely an awareness informed by an understanding of learning styles.

Learning strategies

Learning strategies are patterns of learning behaviour. They are not subject to the same problems as learning styles, being conceptually clear, reliably measured and with clear implications for improving learning. Noel Entwistle and colleagues (e.g. McCune and Entwistle, 2000) have looked at three dimensions of learning strategy: deep learning, surface learning and strategic learning.

The distinction between deep and shallow learning has its roots in 1970s cognitive psychology. In their *levels of processing model* of memory, Craik and Lockhart (1972) distinguished between information that is extensively processed for meaning (i.e. deeply processed) and is well remembered, and that which is processed less extensively for more surface attributes like sound or appearance (shallow processing). Entwistle *et al.* (1989) applied this idea to education, distinguishing between processing academic information for its surface attributes, and study using deep processing strategies. Shallow or *surface* learning involves relying on single sources of information and learning key points by rote. Learners adopting a surface strategy limit what they study and learn to the strict requirements of a syllabus. Deep learning by contrast is characterised by the motivation to understand at as deep a level as possible the material being studied.

■ Box 8.3 Strategies to differentiate by learning style

- ■ Where you have some discretion, avoid wholesale screening for learning style. There may be labelling effects and there is little evidence to suggest that teachers can respond effectively. A specialist can work with concerned individuals.
- ■ Try using images, concept maps and video in resources. This may be of benefit to highly visual learners.
- ■ Use a variety of teaching methods. Although we don't really know that particular teaching methods benefit students with particular learning styles, variety is probably helpful to all.
- ■ Try to think of students in terms of specific strengths and weaknesses – call these learning styles if it is helpful – rather than assign a label based on general ability.
- ■ Consider referring students whose learning style appears to cause them a problem in psychology to a study skills unit.
- ■ Consider offering feedback to students informed by learning styles research – possibly though not necessarily based on their own learning style.

A further dimension of learning strategy concerns how strategic learners are. The strategic learner is effective in organising their time and sources of information. They monitor the effectiveness of their strategies and are adaptable when their achievements do not live up to expectations. Nisbett and Shucksmith (1986) have described strategic learners as having a 'game plan' when approaching an academic task comparable to that of a football team approaching an important match. Box 8.4 shows the characteristics of strategic learning.

Applications of learning strategies research

If students who score highly in strategic and deep learning do better in psychology then it follows that enhancing deep and strategic learning should improve student performance. As a starting point it can certainly be helpful to identify dodgy study habits. However, students over-rely on surface learning as a result of a range of motivational factors. It would be naive then to assume that they can consciously modify these just on the basis of feedback from a learning strategies test. To develop deep learning strategies in learners we would have to impart to them a love of knowledge and thus the intrinsic motivation to study. There are, of course, opportunities to achieve this in psychology, and it is worth remembering that most students choose psychology because they are interested. Currently research into deep learning has been focused on undergraduates, and has found that insight into learning strategy is associated with modest change. McCune and Entwistle (2000) followed up 19 psychology undergraduates over the course of their first year at university, to see whether they managed to modify their learning strategies. It emerged that, although some students made some significant changes, in general learning strategy proved quite difficult to modify.

Strategic learning may be more open to modification than deep learning. Strategic learning can be developed by the use of metacognitive strategies, i.e. approaches to teaching which make clear to students how and why they are learning. This is explicit in vocational courses such as GNVQ and AVCE where learners are regularly required to draw up action plans, name the strategies to be used, gather information and review the task. This 'plan, do and review' approach is closely related to the key activities of strategic learners shown in Box 8.4. Learners can also be taught time management strategies, for example using timetables with

---

■ **Box 8.4 Activities of strategic learners**

- ■ creating a plan of action
- ■ selecting appropriate strategies
- ■ implementing the strategies in order to carry out the plan
- ■ monitoring progress and modifying the strategies or even the plan, as appropriate
- ■ evaluating the outcome to inform future learning experiences.

---

evenings and weekends blocked so that quality study time can be built into the week.

DYSLEXIA

The range of physical and psychological disabilities and difficulties students can bring to their experience of studying psychology is enormous, and there is no room here to explore this range in detail. However dyslexia is a special case because it is so common, and because a lot can be done – but often isn't – to help. First, though, there are a couple of general points to make about dyslexia that apply equally to any specific or pervasive disability or difficulty. First, no one is defined as a person by a difficulty or disability. When we label students during initial assessment processes and make assumptions about what they will be capable of and what strategies will work for them we risk demeaning their individuality. No amount of study of dyslexia or any other difficulty or disability is a substitute for getting to know an individual and building a quality of relationship in which they are comfortable to discuss their particular needs. Second, when we meet a student with dyslexia at any point in their development they will have been shaped by their prior experiences and current circumstances. We are dealing not just with a person with a condition but also with all their acquired habits, preferences and coping strategies. We ignore these at our peril.

A simple example of not incorrect but slightly over-simple advice given to teachers is to provide handouts on yellow paper for students with dyslexia. If you talk to students with dyslexia you soon find that for some people this is helpful but also that for others it makes no difference, that some people prefer a different colour and that some find unjustified formatting, a different font or font size, increased line spacing or pages expanded to A3 to be more helpful. You will also probably meet some students with dyslexia whose priority is to not be identified in lessons by being given distinctive resources or who fiercely defend their ability to cope without special treatment.

Defining dyslexia

The British Dyslexia Association defines dyslexia as follows:

> A specific learning difficulty which mainly affects the development of literacy and language related skills. It is likely to be present at birth and to be lifelong in its effects. It is characterised by difficulties with phonological processing, rapid naming, working memory, processing speed, and the automatic development of skills that may not match up to an individual's other cognitive abilities.

Of course this sort of definition cannot capture the experience of dyslexia. For a moving and instructive account of the journey of two now-successful psychologists with dyslexia I strongly recommend everyone to read Sander and Williamson's (2010) auto-ethnographic analysis. They describe their difficulties in terms of dealing with teachers and employers and the effect of dyslexia on their self-esteem and academic self-confidence. They also point out the often-ignored cognitive strengths associated with dyslexia and the benefits that increased aware-ness of these can have for the self-esteem of dyslexic students.

Using ICT to support students with dyslexia

Dyslexia support is an area where ICT really comes into its own, and there are a number of programs and add-ons that are either designed for or are well-suited to making life easier for students with dyslexia. However, the overlap between specialists in e-learning and special educational needs is quite small, so unfortu-nately you cannot assume that a dyslexic student will be aware of these tools or have access to someone with the specialist skills to show them. Depending on your blend of interpersonal and ICT skills you may actually be the best-equipped profes-sional to do this kind of work. If you are concerned about the ethics of working on the fringes of your competence, keep two principles in mind:

■ Liaise with the relevant specialists. They will probably be very supportive of your efforts and want to develop skills in this area alongside you. As long as you are working with people with complementary skills and knowledge you will probably work out a path that at least does no harm.

■ As long as you are working with students to identify possible strategies for them to try rather than prescribing how they should work, you are very unlikely to do any harm.

Making presentations accessible

The same principles that inform good presentations in general are often *more* important for students with dyslexia. For anyone with working memory problems it is especially important to avoid cognitive overload, therefore avoid excessive sound and animation as well as too much information on a slide. The more blank space and information in non-verbal form the better. There are also some addi-tional variables to consider in dyslexia. One such variable is the contrast ratio between text and background. Normally, high contrast ratios – for example, black on white – are easy to read, but this can lead some students with dyslexia to experi-ence a 'crawling effect' where the text seems to move. Try taking down the contrast ratio to reduce this effect, but not too much or the slides will become hard for everyone to read. You can assess your contrast ratios here: http://snook.ca/tech-nical/colour_contrast/colour.html. The standards referred to on this site are for web design, but the principles apply equally to any medium where text is read from a screen. Another variable to consider in dyslexia is column width; some students with dyslexia may find slides with wide margins easier to read.

Browser settings

When we surf the Internet we are bombarded with imagery, animation and striking text features. Web pages may also feature large volumes of small text that may or may not have a good contrast ratio with the background colour. While all this makes for a rich visual experience it also makes it harder to extract meaning from the page. This is likely to be a particular problem for students with dyslexia. It is possible to make some adjustments, for example to text size, within normal browser settings. However, with a little more exploration we can show students how to exert a lot more control over the way web pages appear to them. Firefox and Internet Explorer both have accessibility add-ons (https://addons.mozilla.org/en-US/firefox/addon/5809/?src=reco and www.paciellogroup.com/resources/wat-ie-about.html respectively). JISC TechDis also produces an excellent plug-in that works with all the major browsers (www.techdis.ac.uk/index.php?p=1_20051905100544) – see Figure 8.1. These toolbars allow you to change text and background colour and to eliminate images and animation from pages. One good tip, however, is to try the less well-known Opera browser instead. This has a number of good accessibility features built in as standard.

Text-to-speech tools

Some people with dyslexia find it easier to process verbal information in auditory form rather than visually. There are some excellent but extremely expensive advanced tools around for converting text to speech and vice versa. Sometimes LEA funding can be used to make these tools available for statemented students. However, there are many students who don't qualify for this but who could potentially benefit from text-to-speech functionality. Basic text-to-speech functions can be found in most operating systems (Narrator in Windows, Orca in Linux, Text-to-speech in Mac). For something a little bit more advanced try Free NaturalReader (www.naturalreaders.com/). To convert text documents to MP3s try Dimio DSpeech (http://dimio.altervista.org/eng/).

You might also want to introduce students to DAISY. DAISY (digital accessibility information systems) is an international standard format designed to make text easier to read. It involves synchronising an audio file with a page so that the reader can follow text on a page while simultaneously listening to it being read. Free DAISY add-ons are available for Microsoft Word (www.daisy.org/project/save-as-daisy-microsoft) and Open Office (http://sourceforge.net/projects/odt2daisy/).

■ **Figure 8.1** The JISC TechDis accessibility toolbar (note the recent rebrand to ATbar)

MOTIVATION

The term 'motivation' can be defined as 'the forces that account for the selection, persistence, intensity and continuation of behaviour' (Snowman and Biehler, 2000: 371). In other words, it is the sum of the influences that affect why we choose to behave in particular ways. A common lament among teachers is that our students are not motivated, but this is technically incorrect: students are always motivated, just not always to do what we want when we want it and in the way we would choose. We can take it though that it is generally in students' interests to work in ways we would recommend. A number of factors influence this. We can look here in particular at two factors, students' self-efficacy and their attributions of success and failure.

Self-efficacy

Self-efficacy refers to our perceptions of our ability to carry out a task (Bandura, 1986). We are concerned here specifically with students' beliefs about their ability to understand and perform well in psychology. This can be independent of more general academic self-efficacy. Students reveal this every time they say 'I'm better at science than psychology' or 'I'm not that clever but I can do psychology'. Schunk (1991) has suggested four sources of information that we draw upon in order to arrive at our academic self-efficacy.

- *Previous experience*: students who have previously succeeded in tasks will generally tend to have higher self-efficacy for related tasks. Thus the psychology student who performs well in a modular exam will be confident of doing so again.
- *Direct persuasion*: feedback to students – formal and informal – can affect their perceptions of their ability to perform tasks.
- *Observational learning*: we tend to pick up on the self-efficacy of our peers. Where students are generally doing well individuals pick up on this and judge their own ability to succeed accordingly.
- *Physiological cues*: we constantly experience our physiological state and use this as a source of information about our current emotional state. If students feel anxious while performing a task they may judge their ability to perform that task as poor.

According to Bandura and his colleagues, the motivation to invest effort in and persist with a task depends on our beliefs about our competence in that task at that moment. Students with high levels of self-efficacy tend to choose more ambitious goals than those with lower levels. They may, for example, set out to master a task rather than merely to attain a minimum acceptable grade. Second, students with high levels of self-efficacy tend to expect more positive outcomes from a task and therefore see fit to invest more effort in achieving it. Finally, people with high self-efficacy tend to be less discouraged by occasional failure because they tend to attribute such failure to insufficient effort rather than lack of ability.

Improving student self-efficacy

There are a number of ways in which psychology teachers can improve the self-efficacy of their students. The general messages given out by teachers in the form of praise and recognition of achievement can help self-efficacy. There are, however, more targeted approaches. One such approach involves goal or target setting. When learners have concrete, realistic short-term goals to work towards, they can judge their self-efficacy in relation to these. There is clear evidence that, when used appropriately, setting goals or targets can enhance performance (see Jarvis, 2005, for a review). Highly explicit outcomes are preferable as they provide solid criteria against which the individual can judge their own achievements. Short-term goals are preferable because they are well remembered at the point where outcome is assessed.

Given the importance of observational learning in self-efficacy beliefs, another avenue to enhancing self-efficacy involves exposing learners to peer success. As nauseating as phrases like 'culture of achievement' can be when used by politicians, it is actually quite true that developing a classroom culture in which a group feels that they are doing well can enhance individuals' self-efficacy. Developing a culture of achievement can be achieved by using sequences of carefully thought-out assessments that are manageable and link closely to recently covered specification content. One rather controversial strategy is to provide false positive feedback. Although empirically validated, this technique raises ethical issues as it means to some extent deceiving students. It is hard as well to reconcile false feedback with helping students develop the metacognitive skills of understanding how they will be assessed. Perhaps a better approach is to focus heavily on skills development and link this to assessment. For example, thinking skills toolkits (see p82) can be used to prepare students for AO2 assessments. This will allow very high levels of genuine success in the assessment.

Attributions of success and failure

Attribution is the cognitive process in which we explain the causes of events. Bernard Weiner (1992) has developed a theory of attribution that has been particularly useful in understanding student motivation. Weiner points out that every time students succeed or fail at a task they attribute this success or failure to a cause. The technical term for this process is *causal inference*. Often we do not have sufficient information to make completely logical causal inferences, but instead rely on general beliefs about the situation and ourselves. These are called *causal schemata*.

Our attributions of success and failure can have a profound effect on our motivation to tackle future tasks. Weiner identified three dimensions to the nature of attributions made by learners regarding success and failure. The first dimension is locus of control. Locus of control refers to the extent to which the individual believes they can control events. Generally, an internal locus of control is more adaptive than an external locus – if we believe we can alter events we tend to be more motivated to tackle them positively.

The second dimension to causality is stability. Causes of success and failure may be stable, i.e. they remain constant across situations (e.g. effort, task difficulty), or they may be unstable, i.e. they change from one situation to another (e.g. luck, mood). The final dimension is controllability. Table 8.2 shows matrix of causal attributions resulting from combinations of controllability, locus of control and stability.

The student with an internal locus of control tends to attribute results to their own actions and characteristics. Where results are judged to be controllable they are attributed to effort. When they are judged to be uncontrollable then ability and mood become the focus of causal inference. On the other hand, the student characterised by an external locus of control tends to attribute their successes and failures to features of the situation. Stable external causes include task difficulty (uncontrollable) and teacher bias (controllable). Unstable causes include luck and unusual help. Table 8.3 shows a range of students' responses to success and failure (adapted from Craske, 1988).

This range of responses can be explained in terms of Weiner's theory. Good and bad 'luck' are external influences, therefore more likely to be attributions made by those with an external locus of control. Luck is also unstable and uncontrollable in nature. If we believe that luck is the primary factor affecting our success or failure we will probably not be motivated to make more effort on future occasions. An attribution of 'I am clever' is somewhat more motivating, being internal rather than external. However, it is also uncontrollable, and where we see results as being beyond our control there is limited motivation to make greater effort. According

■ **Table 8.2** Factors affecting causal attributions of success and failure

Controllability	Internal locus of control		External locus of control	
	stable	unstable	stable	unstable
Controllable	typical effort	atypical effort	teacher bias	atypical help
Uncontrollable	ability	mood	task difficulty	luck

■ **Table 8.3** Examples of causal inferences about success and failure

Success	Failure
'I had good luck'	'I had bad luck'
'It was easy'	'It was too hard'
'I tried hard'	'I didn't try hard enough'
'I am clever'	'I'm not clever enough'

to Weiner the most adaptive type of causal inferences involve effort; when we attribute success and failure to the degree of effort committed to the task we should be maximally motivated to make great effort on future occasions.

Working with student attributions

Attribution theory has a number of important implications for classroom practice. If psychology teachers can identify students who make unhelpful attributions of their successes and failures and work with them to alter these to more positive attributions they should in principle be able to improve their motivation. This can be formalised as a branch of cognitive-behavioural therapy known as *attributional therapy* or be carried out more informally in everyday interaction with learners. Examples of the focus work on attribution might take are shown in Box 8.5.

Occasions arise frequently in the classroom when learners make comments like 'it was easy' in response to success, or 'I'm just not up to this' in response to failure. It can be helpful to challenge these attributions, suggesting for example that in fact a task was not easy, but that the student had in fact put in considerable effort and perhaps demonstrated a talent. This is an example of differentiation by response. Weiner's theory gives us a good basis for understanding how and when to make such challenges. As with all therapeutic techniques, however, this is an art as well as a science; do not throw out your experience and common sense and embrace techniques like attribution too religiously. The principle underlying all cognitive techniques is that the current beliefs are in some way incorrect. It is thus helpful for learners to attribute failure to lack of effort *provided they did not actually make sufficient effort*. However, it is quite possible for students to make considerable effort and to fall foul of bad luck in exam questions or poor marking, and nothing could be more demotivating than to be told it was a result of lack of effort (Marshall, 1990). In such cases it may be more helpful to agree that the learner was unlucky and focus on the likelihood that next time they will probably have better luck.

■ **Box 8.5 Examples of alterations in learner attributions**

Uncontrollable → controllable attributions — e.g. ability → effort.
External → internal attributions — e.g. luck → effort.
Stable → unstable attributions — e.g. potential → mood

GENDER

At GCSE and A-level female students achieve marginally better grades than males across the board. This disparity is much greater in psychology than in most subjects. Table 8.4 shows the gendered 2005 A-level grade distribution of psychology (all boards combined) in comparison with grades across all subjects.

■ **Table 8.4** AS cumulative grade distribution by gender (Source: JCQ)

Gender	A		B		C		D		E	
	2009	2008	2009	2008	2009	2008	2009	2008	2009	2008
Psychology M	7.9	7.7	21.2	21.3	40.2	40.1	59.5	59.4	77.1	76
F	14.8	15	32.6	33.5	53	53.8	70.6	71.1	83.4	84.3
All subjects M	18.3	17.2	35.8	34.9	55.6	54.9	73.1	72.9	86.3	86.2
F	20.5	19.9	40.9	40.2	61.5	61.6	78.3	78.6	89.9	89.1

While the gender disparity across all subjects is modest, it is considerably greater in psychology, with A–C achievement in males being only 40.2% as opposed to 53% for females. For many psychologists, gender is synonymous with feminism (Nicolson, 1997), and when we discuss gender differences we are almost always focusing on the ways in which women are disadvantaged. While feminist commentators are quite correct to point out that nobody identified a crisis in the past when male achievement outstripped female (Francis and Skelton, 2001), we have a responsibility for all students and so we find ourselves in the unusual position of trying to enhance the attainment of males relative to that of females. Although this may make us uncomfortable, there is essentially no conflict between saying, on one hand, that much traditional psychology marginalises the characteristics, needs and experiences of women, and, on the other, that currently male students underachieve relative to female students. These are separate issues and each can be addressed without diminishing the importance of the other.

So why do boys underachieve? Younger *et al.* (2005) have identified the following possible factors:

■ Neurological differences between male and female brains leading to different patterns of information processing.
■ Cultural norms of masculinity that involve disregard for achievement and authority.
■ Lower aspirations among male students.
■ Greater maturity and better social skills and learning strategies in female students.
■ Different quality of interactions of male and female students with peers and teachers.

They suggest that tackling these generic problems requires intervention on four levels:

■ *Pedagogic*: classroom-based approaches centred on teaching and learning.
■ *Individual*: effective use of target setting and mentoring.
■ *Organisational*: ways of organising learning at the whole-school level.

■   *Socio-cultural*: approaches that attempt to create an environment for learning where key boys and girls feel able to work with the aims and aspirations of the institution.

Subject-specific factors: is psychology a feminine subject?

Not to discount the potential importance of generic factors affecting male achievement, but given that gender differences in achievement are greater in psychology than in most subjects, we should also consider the possibility that subject-specific factors are at work. One angle on this is to consider the differential achievement in different school subjects at secondary level. Boys do well in maths and science, less so in arts subjects. If psychology were actually as scientific and mathematical as it is often represented we might suppose that boys would have the advantage rather than girls. Clearly this is not the case.

Based on this we might cautiously propose that emphasising the 'hard science' and statistical aspects of psychology may advantage boys. Note that currently this is not empirically validated but represents a logical strategy. There may, for example, be parts of the psychology curriculum that are seen as traditionally feminine that can be enhanced for boys by inserting some 'hard science'. For example, primary caregiver–infant attachment and day care may be to some extent masculinised by emphasising methodological analysis of some key studies and by making reference to contemporary neuroscience, which has examined the effect of privation on brain development.

Topic options may provide another opportunity to cater for masculine interests. Specifications with applied options such as sport and criminal psychology make this more straightforward. Examples and resources offered to students may also be differentially appealing to boys and girls. Take for example social learning. Where this fits into the curriculum varies according to what specification is being followed, but social learning is often framed as a way of explaining children's developing behaviour – a 'feminine' area of psychology. By introducing the current debates about the effects of modelled aggression in televised football this can be made equally relevant to both genders.

CONCLUSIONS AND REFLECTIONS

We have come a long way in realizing that recognising and trying in good faith to meet the varying needs of our students is central to the teacher role. In the classroom of the 21st century differentiation means having the resources, tasks, support systems and feedback that take account of the differing needs of individual students. In terms of cognitive variables you might want to consider how students vary in terms of intelligence and academic ability – take care not to confuse these ideas – learning style and dyslexia. A word of caution is always needed when talking about learning styles. Although learning styles in the broadest sense exist, the term has been devalued by several conceptual and practical problems, and we should be extremely cautious about some of the recommendations made by producers of commercial learning styles assessments packages. If we use a variety of teaching methods and make suggestions to individuals based on their individual strengths and weaknesses then we are differentiating by learning styles. There is quite a lot we can do to help students with dyslexia but remember that dyslexic students vary considerably, both in terms of how they process information and in terms of their emotional responses and coping strategies.

Students differ as well in terms of sociocognitive variables such as motivation and gender. It is possible to enhance motivation by boosting self-efficacy and by manipulating attributions of success and failure. Although it is well established that girls significantly outperform boys in psychology and, despite the wealth of research into gender differences in general achievement, it remains unclear why boys are so disadvantaged in psychology. As well as the general types of strategy used to boost male achievement it may be possible to masculinise elements of the psychology curriculum.

One final word about 'differentiation'. The word often strikes terror into the hearts of teachers who fear that they are somehow meant to be providing tailor-made resources and activities for every student in every lesson. Forget it, or at least forget the idea that that level of personalisation comes as standard or is sustainable indefinitely. If you are producing user-friendly resources, making good use of ICT, making use of peer interaction, offering individualised feedback and using an appropriate range of examples in teaching then you are already differentiating. You can supplement this with targeting particular strategies to individuals as you get to know them.

QUESTIONS FOR REFLECTION

1   Do you tend to see fairness more in terms of treating students the same or more in terms of meeting their individual needs?
2   How much do you know about the individual needs of your students? Do you encourage them to discuss these with you?
3   Do you tend to think in terms of students in terms of a fixed ability or in terms of developing their skills?
4   How much do you know about dyslexia?
5   Do you consider student motivation when you give feedback or do you tend to think more about the fit between their answers and the assessments they are preparing for?
6   Do you take account of gender issues in your teaching?

NOTE

1   Sexism in psychology is not within the scope of this chapter. See the 1997 special issue of *Psychology Teaching* for further information.

FURTHER READING

Francis, B. and Skelton, C. (2001) *Investigating gender: contemporary perspectives in educa-tion*. Buckingham, Open University Press.

Jarvis, M. (2005) *The psychology of effective learning and teaching*. Cheltenham, Nelson Thornes.

Riding, R. J. and Rayner, S. (1998) *Cognitive styles and learning strategies*. London, David Fulton.

Taylor, J. and Trapp, A. (Eds) (2010) Special issue: widening participation in psychology. *Psychology Teaching Review* **16**, 1–110.

Younger, M., Warrington, M., Gray, J., Rudduck, J., McLellan, R., Bearne, E., Kershner, R. and Bricheno, P. (2005) *Raising boys' achievement*. London, DfES.

APPENDICES

APPENDIX I

Publishers specialising in post-16 psychology

Collins
77–85 Fulham Palace Road
London
W6 8JB
www.collins.co.uk

Heinemann Educational
FREEPOST (OF1771)
PO Box 381
Oxford
OX2 8BR
www.heinemann.co.uk

Hodder Headline
338 Euston Road
London
NW1 3BH
http://www.hodderheadline.co.uk/
index.asp?area=ed

Nelson Thornes Ltd
Delta Place
27 Bath Road
Cheltenham
Glos
GL53 7TH
www.nelsonthornes.com

Oxford University Press
Great Clarendon Street
Oxford
OX2 7TW
http://www.oup.co.uk/oxed/
secondary/

Palgrave Macmillan
Houndmills
Basingstoke
Hampshire
RG21 6XS
www.palgrave.com

Philip Allan Updates
Market Place
Deddington
Oxon
OX15 0SE
www.philipallan.co.uk

Psychology Press
27 Church Road
Hove
East Sussex
BN3 2FA
www.psypress.co.uk

APPENDIX II

Professional bodies that support psychology teaching

The Association for the Study of Animal Behaviour (ASAB)
141 Newmarket Road
Cambridge
CB5 8HA
http://asab.nottingham.ac.uk/

The Association for the Teaching of Psychology (ATP)
c/o The British Psychological
Society
St Andrews House
48 Princess Road East
Leicester
LE1 7DR
http://theatp.org/

The British Psychological Society (BPS)
St Andrews House
48 Princess Road East
Leicester
LE1 7DR
www.bps.org.uk

The Society for the Teaching of Psychology (STP)
Le Moyne College
Syracuse
NY 13214
http://teachpsych.lemoyne.edu/
teachpsych/div/divindex.html

The National Institute on the Teaching of Psychology (NITOP)
2303 Naples Court
Champaign
IL 61822
www.nitop.org

Teachers of Psychology in Secondary Schools (TOPSS)
Education Directorate
750 First Street, NE
Washington
DC 20002-4242
http://www.apa.org/ed/topss/
homepage.html

The European Federation of Psychology Teaching Associations (EFPTA)
www.efpta.org

APPENDIX III

Journals specialising in the teaching of psychology

Essays from E-xcellence in Teaching
Produced by the Society for the Teaching of Psychology
Available free online
http://teachpsych.lemoyne.edu/teachpsych/eit/index.html

Psychology Learning & Teaching
Produced by the Higher Education Academy
Available free online
http://www.psychology.heacademy.ac.uk/html/plat_journal.asp

Psychology Teacher Network
Produced by TOPSS
Current issue free online
http://www.apa.org/ed/topss/homepage.html

ATP Today
Produced by the Association for the Teaching of Psychology
Free to members
http://www.theatp.org/topics/magazine

Psychology Teaching Review
Produced by the British Psychological Society Division for Teachers & Researchers in Psychology.
Free to DTRP members

Teaching of Psychology
Produced by the Society for the Teaching of Psychology
Free to members
http://www.informaworld.com/smpp/title~content=t775653707~tab=subscribe

e-Journal of Psychology Teaching
Produced by the Psychology Teacher Training Network
Available free online
http://journal.psychologyteaching.org/

APPENDIX IV

Awarding bodies offering post-16 psychology qualifications

AQA
GCSE, A-level, Access to HE,
AEA
Stag Hill House
Guildford, Surrey
GU2 7XJ
www.aqa.org.uk

Edexcel
A-level
One90 High Holborn
London
WC1V 7BH
www.edexcel.org.uk/home

International Baccalaureate
IB Diploma
Johannesgatan 20
Stockholm
SE-11138
SWEDEN
www.internationalbaccalaureate.
co.uk

NOCN
Access to HE
9 St James Court
Friar Gate
Derby
DE1 1BT
www.nocn.org.uk

OCR
GCSE, A-level
OCR
Westwood Business Park
Westwood Way
Coventry
CV4 8JQ
www.ocr.org.uk

SQA
Scottish Higher
24 Douglas Street
Glasgow
G2 7NQ
www.sqa.org.uk

WJEC
WJEC
245 Western Avenue
Cardiff
CF5 2YX
www.wjec.co.uk

REFERENCES

Alloway, T., Wilson, G., Graham, J. and Krames, L. (2000) *Sniffy the virtual rat – Lite version*. Berlmont, Thomson Learning.

Allport, A. (1980) Patterns and actions: cognitive mechanisms are content-specific. In Claxton, G.L. (ed.) *Cognitive psychology: new directions*. London, Routledge & Kegan Paul.

Ausubel, D.P. (1968) *Educational psychology: a cognitive view*. New York, Holt.

Balch, W.R. (2005) Elaborations of introductory psychology terms: effects on test performance and subjective ratings. *Teaching of Psychology* **32**, 29–33.

Bandura, A. (1986) *Social foundations of thought and action*. Englewood Cliffs NJ, Prentice Hall.

Bandura, M. and Dweck, C.S. (1981) The relationship of conceptions of intelligence and achievement goals to achievement-related cognition, affect and behaviour. Unpublished manuscript, Harvard University.

Banister, P. (2003) Impact of post-16 qualifications on the undergraduate curriculum: views from Heads of Psychology Departments. In McGuinness, C. (ed.) *Post-16 qualifications in psychology*. Leicester, British Psychological Society.

Barkham, M. and Mellor-Clark, J. (2000) Rigour and relevance: the role of practice-based evidence in the psychological therapies. In Rowland, N. and Goss, S. (eds) *Evidence-based counselling and psychological therapies*. London, Routledge.

BECTA (2003) *ICT research*. www.becta.org.uk/research.

Blair-Broeker, C. (2002) Bringing psychology to life. *Essays from e-xcellence in teaching* **2**, np.

Blass, T. and Schmitt, C. (2001) The nature of perceived authority in the Milgram paradigm: Two replications. *Current Psychology* **20**, 115–21.

Bloom, B.S. (ed.) (1956) *Taxonomy of educational objectives: The classification of educational goals*, Handbook I, *Cognitive Domain*. McKay, New York.

Bolam, P. (2004) A case study on the development and use of an e-learning initiative. *Psychology Teaching* **Summer**, 39–45.

Bowman, L.L. and Waite, B.M. (2003) Volunteering in research: student satisfaction and educational benefits. *Teaching of Psychology* **30**, 102–6.

British Psychological Society (1997) *The Division for Teachers & Researchers in Psychology: about us*. http://www.bps.org.uk/sub-sites$/dtrp/about.cfm.

British Psychological Society (2009a) *Code of ethics and conduct*. Leicester, British Psychological Society.

British Psychological Society (2009b) *Ethical principles for conducting research with human participants*. Leicester, British Psychological Society.

Burden, B. (1993) Psychology and cinema. In Rose, D. and Radford, J. (eds) *Teaching psychology: information and resources*. Leicester, BPS Books.

Burns, A. (1998) Pop psychology or Ken behaving badly. *The Psychologist* **11** (7), 360.

Carlsmith, K.M. and Cooper, J. (2002) A persuasive example of collaborative learning. *Teaching of Psychology* **29**, 132–5.

Churach, D. and Fisher, D. (2001) Science students surf the web: effects on constructivist classroom environments. *Journal of Computers in Mathematics and Science Teaching*, **20**, 221–47.

Clarke, C. (2004) Secretary of State for Education. Available at www.becta.org.uk/corporate/index.cfm. Accessed 9 February 2004.

Coffield, F. and Edward, S. (2009) Rolling out 'good', 'best' and 'excellent' practice: what's next, perfect practice? *British Journal of Educational Research* **35**, 371–90.

Coffield, F., Moseley, D., Hall, E. and Ecclestone, K. (2004) *Should we be using learning styles? What research has to say to practice*. Learning and Skills Development Agency.

Cohen, J. (2004) Parasocial break-up from favourite television characters: the role of attachment styles and relationship intensity. *Journal of Social & Personal Relationships* **21**, 187–202.

Conway, M. and Banister, P. (2007) High quality science A-level: good for students, universities and the discipline. *The Psychologist* **20**, 608–9.

Cook, J.L. (2005) Constructing knowledge: the value of teaching from multiple perspectives. Paper delivered at the NITOP annual conference.

Craik, F.I.M. and Lockhart, R.S. (1972) Levels of processing: a framework for memory research. *Journal of Verbal Learning and Verbal Behaviour* **11**, 671–84.

Crandall, C.S., Eshleman, A. and O'Brien, L. (2002) Social norms and the expression and suppression of prejudice: The struggle for internalization. *Journal of Personality and Social Psychology* **82**, 359–78.

Craske, M. (1988) Learned helplessness, self-worth motivation and attribution retraining for primary school children. *British Journal of Educational Psychology* **58**, 152–64.

Dahlgren, M. and Dahlgren, L. (2002) Portraits of PBL: students' experiences of the characteristics of PBL in physiotherapy, computer engineering and psychology. *Instructional Science* **30**, 111–27.

Daniel, D.B. (2005) Using Powerpoint to ruin a perfectly good lecture. Paper presented to the 1st Biennial SCRD Teaching of Developmental Science Institute. August 2005.

Dickson, K.L., Miller, M.D. and Devoley, M.S. (2005) Effect of textbook study guides on student performance in introductory psychology. *Teaching of Psychology* **32**, 34–9.

Dickson, N. (2010) The application of problem-based learning in the psychology A-level classroom. *e-Journal of Psychology Teaching* **1**, 16–22.

Dietz-Uhler, B. and Lanter, J.R. (2009) Using the four-questions technique to enhance learning. *Teaching of Psychology* **46**, 38–41.

Diseth, A. (2002) The relationship between intelligence, learning styles, approaches to learning and academic achievement. *Scandinavian Journal of Educational Research* **46**, 219–30.

Dobson, C. (2008) *Conducting research with people not having the capacity to consent to their participation*. Leicester, British Psychological Society.

Dodge, B. (1995) *Some thoughts about webquests*. http://webquest.sdsu.edu/about_webquests.html. Last accessed 28 September 2010.

Dunn, J. and Munn, P. (1985) Becoming a family member: family conflict and the development of social understanding in the first year. *Child Development* **50**, 306–18.

Dweck, C.S. (2000) *Self-theories: Their role in motivation, personality and development*. Philadelphia PA, Psychology Press.

Dweck, C.S., Chiu, C. and Hong, Y. (1995) Implicit theories and their role in judgments and reactions: a world from two perspectives. *Psychological Inquiry* **6**, 267–85.

Eide, E., Goldhaber, D. and Brewer, D. (2004) The teacher labour market and teacher quality. *Oxford Review of Economic Policy* **20**, 230–44.

Entwistle, N.J., Hounsell, D., Macaulay, C., Situnayke, G. and Tait, H. (1989) *The performance of electrical engineering students in Scottish higher education*. Final report to the Scottish Education Department. Edinburgh, University of Edinburgh.

Facione, P.E. (1995) The California Critical Thinking Skills Test. www.insightassessment.com

Facione, P.E. and Facione, N.C. (1994) *Holistic critical thinking scoring rubric*. Milbrae, California Academic Press.

Faria, L. (1998) Personal conceptions of intelligence, attributions and school achievement: development of a comprehensive model of inter-relations during adolescence. *Psicologia: Revista da Associacao Psicologia* **12**, 101–13.

Faria, L. and Fontaine, A. M. (1997) Adolescents' personal conceptions of intelligence: the development of a new scale and some exploratory evidence. *European Journal of Psychology of Education* **12**, 51–62.

Felder, R.M. and Silverman, L.K. (1988) Learning and teaching styles in engineering education. *Engineering Education* **78**, 674–81.

Fisher, R. (1995) *Teaching Children to Think*. Cheltenham, Glos., Nelson Thornes.

Fitz-Gibbon, C.T. and Vincent, L. (1994) *Candidates' performance in science and mathematics at A-level*. London, SCAA.

Flavell, J.H. (1985) *Cognitive development*. Englewood Cliffs NJ, Prentice Hall.

Francis, B. and Skelton, C. (2001) *Investigating gender: contemporary perspectives in education*. Buckingham, Open University Press.

Gage, N.L. and Berliner, D.C. (1991) *Educational psychology*. Boston, Houghton Mifflin.

Geher, G., Bauman, K.P., Hubbard, S.E.K. and Legare, J.R. (2002) Self and other obedience estimates: biases and moderators. *Journal of Social Psychology* **142**, 677–89.

Gorenflo, D.W. and McConnell, J.V. (1991) The most frequently cited journal articles and authors in introductory psychology textbooks. *Teaching of Psychology* **18**, 8–12.

Gove, M. (2010) *Secretary of State for Education speech to the National College Annual Conference*. National College 2010.

Grant, F. (2004) Free statistics software: Yours, free to keep. *Scientific Computing* **October**, np.

Green, R.J. (2005) Teaching psychology through film, video. American Psychological Society. Retrieved from www.psychologicalscience.org/teaching/tips/tips_0703.cfm

Green, S. (2007) The cookbook approach: a recipe for disaster? *The Psychologist* **20**, 610–11.

Gregorc, A.F. (1979). Learning/teaching styles: Potent forces behind them. *Educational Leadership* **36**, 234–6.

Griggs, R.A. and Marek, P. (2001) Similarity of introductory psychology textbooks: reality or illusion. *Teaching of Psychology* **28**, 254–6.

Grigorenko, E.L., Jarvin, L. and Sternberg, R.J., (2002) School-based tests of the triarchic theory of intelligence: three settings, three samples, three syllabi. *Contemporary Educational Psychology* **27**, 167–208.

Gurung, R.A.R. (2003) Pedagogical aids and student performance. *Teaching of Psychology* **30**, 92–5.

Gurung, R.A.R. (2004) Pedagogical aids: learning enhancers or dangerous detours? *Teaching of Psychology* **31**, 164–6.

Guskey, T.R. (2007) Leadership in the age of accountability. *Educational Horizons,* **Fall**, 29–34.

Haworth, G. (1997) *Using ATP software to teach psychology*. Proceedings of the 15th ATP Conference. University of Surrey July 1997, 126–8.

Hirschler, S. and Banyard, P. (2003) Post-16 students: views and experiences of studying psychology. In McGuinness, C. (ed.) *Post-16 qualifications in psychology*. Leicester, British Psychological Society.

Howitt, D. and Owusu-Bempah, K. (1994) *The racism of psychology: time for change*. Hemel Hempstead, Harvester Wheatsheaf.

International Union of Psychological Science (2008) *Universal declaration of ethical principles for psychologists*. Berlin, IUPS.

Jackson, S.L., Griggs, R.A., Koenig, C.S., Christopher, A.N. and Marek, P. (2000) *A compendium of introductory psychology texts: 1997–2000*. Lemoyne, Office of Teaching Resources for Psychology.

Jarvis, M. (2001) *Angles on child psychology*. Cheltenham, Nelson Thornes.

Jarvis, M. (2000) Teaching psychodynamic psychology: from discourse analysis towards a model of reflective practice. *Psychology Teaching* **8**, 13–21.

Jarvis, M. (2003) Survey of psychology teachers' views on continual professional development. In McGuinness, C. (ed.) *Post-16 qualifications in psychology*. Leicester, British Psychological Society.

Jarvis, M. (2004) The rigour and appeal of psychology A-level. *Education Today* **54**, 24–8.

Jarvis, M. (2005) *The psychology of effective learning and teaching*. Cheltenham, Nelson Thornes.

Jarvis, M. (2006a) Learning strategies and AS-level achievement: an exploratory study. Paper presented at the Annual Conference of the European Learning Styles Information Network. 11 June 2006, University of Oslo.

Jarvis, M. (2006b) *Moments of transition and the exercise of vital powers: crisis and opportunity in the future of psychology teaching*. Paper presented at the 'It may be psychology but not as we know it' conference. September, Manchester Metropolitan University.

Jarvis, M. (2007) Who nurtures the nurturer? CPD and the psychology teacher. *The Psychologist* **20**, 614–6.

Jarvis, M. (2010) Informing the psychology teaching research agenda: who is doing what in related professions? *e-Journal of Psychology Teaching* **1**, 2–7.

Jarvis, M., Russell, J. and Gorman, P. (2004) *Angles on psychology*. 2nd edition. Cheltenham, Nelson Thornes.

JISC (2008) *Exploring tangible benefits of e-learning: does investment yield interest?* JISC, Northumbria University.

Karau, S.J. and Williams, K.D. (1993) Social loafing: a meta-analytic review. *Journal of Personality & Social Psychology* **65**, 681–706.

Kelly, G.A. (1955) *The psychology of personal constructs*. New York, Norton.

Kimble, G.A. (1999) Functional behaviourism: a plan for the unity of psychology. Invited address presented at the annual meetings of the American Psychological Association, Boston.

Kinchin, I.M. (2006) Increasing the accessibility of PowerPoint presentations for those students who do not favour serialist learning styles and/or rote memorisation, European Learning Styles Information Network (ELSIN) 11th Annual Conference, 12–14 June, Oslo, Norway.

Kuwar, B. (2010) Using the four questions technique in A-level psychology teaching to enhance learning. *e-Journal of Psychology Teaching* **1**, 8–15.

Larkin, M. (2002) Using scaffolding instruction to optimize learning. *ERIC Digest*.

Lavender, A., Thompson, L. and Burns, S. (2003) Training and staff retention: National issues and findings from the South Thames (Salomons) Clinical Psychology Training Scheme. *Clinical Psychology* **21**, 20–6.

Leafe, D. (2001) Intranets: developing a learning community. In Leask, M. (ed.) *Issues in teaching using ICT*. Routledge Falmer, London.

Lee, V.S. (2004) *Teaching and learning through enquiry*. Virginia, Stylus Publishing.

Leeming, F.C. (2002) The exam-a-day procedure improves performance in psychology classes. *Teaching of Psychology* **29**, 210–12.

Levy, S., Stroessner, S. and Dweck, C. (1998) Stereotype formation and endorsement: the role of implicit theories. *Journal of Personality & Social Psychology* **74**, 1421–36.

Linnell, M. (2003) Second year undergraduate psychology students: views on their study of post-16 psychology. In McGuinness, C. (ed.) *Post-16 qualifications in psychology*. Leicester, British Psychological Society.

Learning and Skills Council (2004) *National learner satisfaction survey FE 2002-3*. Learning and Skills Council.

Luiten, J., Ames, W. and Ackerman, G. (1980) A meta-analysis of the effects of advance organisers on learning and retention. *American Educational Research Journal* **17**, 211–82.

Maag, M. (2004) The effectiveness of interactive multimedia learning tool on nursing students' math knowledge and self-efficacy. *Computers, Informatics, Nursing* **22**, 26–33.

McCune, V. and Entwistle, N. (2000) *The deep approach to learning: analytic abstraction and idiosyncratic development*. Paper presented at the Innovations in Higher Education Conference, Helsinki.

McGhee, P. (2001) *Thinking psychologically*. Basingstoke, Palgrave.

McGuinness, C. (1999) *From thinking skills to thinking classrooms*. London, Department for Education and Employment.

McGuinness, C. (ed.) (2003) *Post-16 qualifications in psychology*. Leicester, British Psychological Society.

McLoughlin, C. and Lee, M.J.W. (2007) *Social software and participatory learning: pedagogical choices with technology affordances in the web2.0 era*. Proceedings of ASCILITE, Singapore 2007.

Maki, R., Maki, W.S., Patterson, M. and Whittaker, P.D. (2000) Evaluation of a web-based introductory psychology course: 1. Learning and satisfaction in on-line versus lecture courses. *Behaviour Research Methods, Instruments & Computers* **32**, 230–9.

Maras, P. and Bradshaw, V. (2007) *A-level psychology: exploring the views of pre-tertiary psychology teachers*. London, Greenwich University.

Marek, P., Griggs, R.A. and Christopher, A.N. (1999) Pedagogical aids in textbooks: do college students' perceptions justify their prevalence? *Teaching of Psychology* **26**, 11–19.

Marshall, S.P. (1990) *What students learn and remember from word instruction*. Paper presentation at the annual meeting of the American Educational Research Association, Boston.

Mayo, J.A. (2004) Repertory grid as a means to compare and contrast developmental theorists. *Teaching of Psychology* **31**, 178–80.

Meyers, S.A. (1997) Increasing student participation and productivity in small-group activities for psychology classes. *Teaching of Psychology* **24**, 105–15.

Morris, P. (2003) Not the soft option. *The Psychologist* **16**, 510–11.

Mottarella, K., Fritzche, B. and Parrish, T. (2005) Who learns more? Achievement scores following web-based versus classroom instruction in psychology courses. *Psychology Learning & Teaching* **4**, 51–4.

National Learning Network (2004) Learning technologies. Available at www.ccm.ac.uk/ltech/ilt/default.asp. Accessed 9 February 2004.

Naylor, R. and Smith, J. (2002) *Schooling effects on subsequent university performance: evidence from the current university population*. Warwick, Warwick University.

Nevid, J.S. and Lampmann, J.L. (2003) Effects on content acquisition of signalling key concepts in text material. *Teaching of Psychology* **30**, 227–30.

Nicolson, P. (1997) Gender and psychology: adding gender to the curriculum. *Psychology Teaching* **5**, 13–18.

Nisbett, J. and Shucksmith, J. (1986) *Learning strategies*. Routledge & Kegan Paul, London.

Norton, L. (2004) *Psychology applied learning scenarios (PALS): a practical introduction to problem-based learning using vignettes for psychology lecturers*. York, Learning and Teaching Support Network.

Norvig, P. (2003) *The Gettysburg PowerPoint presentation*. http://norvig.com/Gettysburg/. Last accessed 28 September 2010.

Nummedal, S.G., Benson, J.B. and Chew, S.L. (2002) Disciplinary styles in the scholarship of learning and teaching: a view from psychology. In Huber, M.T. and Morreale, S.P.

(eds) *Disciplinary styles in the scholarship of learning and teaching: exploring common ground.* Washington DC, American Association for Higher Education.

Ocampo, C., Prieto, L.R., Whittlesey, V., Connor, J., Janco-Gidley, J., Mannix, S. and Sare, K. (2003) Diversity research in *Teaching of Psychology*: summary and recommendations. *Teaching of Psychology* **30**, 5–18.

Ofsted (2009) *Virtual learning environment: an evaluation of their development in a sample of educational settings.* London, Ofsted.

Oley, N. (2002) Extra credit and peer tutoring: impact on the quality of writing in introductory psychology in an open admissions college. In Griggs, R.A. (ed.) *Handbook for teaching introductory psychology* vol 3. Mahwah NJ, Lawrence Erlbaum Associates.

Palmer, S. (2003) Enquiry based learning can maximise a student's potential. *Psychology Learning & Teaching* **2**, 82–6.

Papert, S. (1996) *The connected family: Bridging the digital generation gap.* Atlanta GA, Longstreet Press.

Pennington, H. (2000) Can American introductory textbooks help us teach critical thinking about psychology? *Psychology Teaching* **8**, 22–4.

Perkins, D.V. and Saris, R.N. (2001) A jigsaw classroom technique for undergraduate statistics courses. *Teaching of Psychology* **28**, 111–13.

Perlman, B. and McCann, L.I. (1999) Developing teaching portfolios. Workshop presented at the Mid-America Conference for Teachers of Psychology. Evansville IN.

Pheiffer, G., Andrew, D., Green, M. and Holley, D. (2003) The role of learning styles in integrating and empowering learners. *Investigations in University Teaching & Learning* **1**, 36–9.

Philo, G., Secker, J., Henderson, L., McLaughlin, G. and Burnside, J. (1994) The impact of the mass media on public images of mental illness: media content and audience belief. *Health Education Journal* **53**, 271–81.

QCA (2006) *GCE AS and A-level criteria for science.* London, QCA.

Rammel, B. and Haysom, M. (2006) *Forward to Framework for Excellence.* Coventry, Learning and Skills Council.

Reynolds, M. (1997) Learning styles: a critique. *Management Learning* **28**, 115–33.

Rice, M. and Brooks, R. (2004) *Developmental dyslexia in adults: a review.* London, National Research and Development Centre for Adult Numeracy & Literacy.

Riding, R. (1991) *Cognitive styles analysis.* Birmingham, Learning & Training Technology.

Riding, R. J. and Rayner, S. (1998) *Cognitive styles and learning strategies.* London, David Fulton.

Rivkin, S.J., Hanushek, E.A. and Kain, J.F. (2005) Teachers, schools and academic achievement. *Econometrica* **73**, 417–58.

Rowley, M. and Dalgarno, L. (2010) A-level psychology teachers: who are they and what do they think about psychology as a subject and as a discipline? Paper delivered at the Annual Conference of the Association for the Teaching of Psychology, July 2010, University of Keele.

Ruscio, J. (2001) Administering quizzes at random to increase students' reading. *Teaching of Psychology* **28**, 204–6.

Rust, J. and Golombok, S. (1999) *Modern psychometrics.* London, Routledge.

Sander, P. and Williamson, S. (2010) Our teachers and what we have learnt from them. *Psychology Teaching Review* **16**.

Sappington, J., Kinsey, K. and Munasayac, K. (2002) Two studies of reading compliance among college students. *Teaching of Psychology* **29**, 272–4.

Schon, D.A. (1983) *The reflective professional: How professionals think in action.* Aldershot, Hants, Avebury.

Schon, D.A. (1987) *Educating the reflective practitioner.* San Francisco, Jossey Bass Wiley.

Schunk, D.H. (1991) Self-efficacy and academic motivation. *Educational Psychologist* **26**, 207–32.

Sellinger, M. (2001) The role of the teacher: teacherless classrooms? In Leask, M. (ed.) *Issues in teaching using ICT*. London, Routledge Falmer.

Selwyn, N. (2007) Web2.0 applications as alternative environments for informal learning: a critical review. Paper delivered at OECD-KERIS expert meeting.

Shapiro, D. (2002) Reviewing the scientist-practitioner model. *The Psychologist* **15**, 232–4.

Shulman, L.S. (1986) Those who understand: a conception of teacher knowledge. *American Educator* **10**, 9–15.

Sizer, T.R. (1992) *Horace's compromise: the dilemma of the American High School*. Boston, Houghton Mifflin.

Smith, S.M. and Woody, P.C. (2000) Interactive effect of multimedia instruction and learning styles. *Teaching of Psychology* **27**, 220–3.

Snowman, J. and Biehler, R. (2000) *Psychology applied to teaching*. Boston, Houghton-Mifflin.

Sternberg, R.J. (1997) What does it mean to be smart? *Educational Leadership* **54**, 20–4.

Sternberg, R.J. (1999) A comparison of three models for teaching psychology. *Psychology Teaching Review* **8**, 37–43.

Sternberg, R.J. and Clinkenbeard, P.R. (1995) A triarchic model for identifying, teaching and assessing gifted children. *Roeper Review* **17**, 255–60.

Sternberg, R.J., Torff, B. and Grigorenko, E.L. (1998) Teaching triarchically improves school achievement. *Journal of Educational Psychology* **90**, 1–11.

Sternberg, R.J. and Grigorenko, E.L. (1999) In praise of dilettantism. *APS Observer* **12**, 37–8.

Suri, H. and Schuhmacher, M. (2008) Open-source vs proprietary VLE: An exploratory study of staff perceptions. Paper presented at accilite. Melbourne, 2008.

Sutton, J. (2006) Future directions for psychology teaching. *The Psychologist* **19**, 68–9.

Taylor, J. and Trapp, A. (eds) (2010) Special issue: widening participation in psychology. *Psychology Teaching Review* **16**, 1–110.

Tharp, R.G. and Gallimore, R. (1991) A theory of teaching as assisted performance. In Light, P., Sheidon, S. and Littleton, K. (eds) *Learning to think*. London, Routledge.

Tombs, S. (2004) Writing, arguing and evaluation – the perspective from Higher Education. *Psychology Teaching* **Summer**, 36–8.

Torgerson, S.J., Torgerson, D.J. Birks, Y.F. and Porthouse, J. (2005) A comparison of random control trials in health and education. *British Educational Research Journal* **31**, 761–85.

Tufte, E. (2004) PowerPoint is evil. *Wired* **9**, np.

Usher, R., Bryant, I. and Johnston, R. (1997) *Adult education and the postmodern challenge: Learning beyond the limits*. London, Routledge.

Velmans, M., Morrison, L., Colley, A., Foot, H., Foreman, N., Kent, G., Kwiatkowski, R. and Sloboda, J. (2004) *Guidelines for minimum standards of ethical approval in psychological research*. Leicester, British Psychological Society.

Venneman, S.S. and Knowles, L.R. (2005) Sniffing out efficacy: Sniffy Lite, a virtual animal lab. *Teaching of Psychology* **32**, 66–8.

Vidal-Abarca, E. and Sanjose, V. (1998) Levels of comprehension of scientific prose: the role of text variables. *Learning & Instruction* **8**, 215–33.

Walker, K.(2004) Why do sixth form students choose psychology? A report of research in one institution. *Psychology Teaching* **Summer**, 29–35.

Weiner, B. (1992) *Human motivation: Metaphors, theories and research*. Thousand Oaks CA, Sage.

Williams, R.L., Oliver, R., Allin, J.L., Winn, B.and Booher, C.S. (2003) Psychological critical thinking as a course predictor and outcome variable. *Teaching of Psychology* **30**, 220–3.

Wilson, V. (2000) *Educational forum on teaching thinking skills*. Edinburgh, Scottish Executive Education Department.

Witkin, H.A. (1964) Origins or cognitive style. In Sheerer, C. (ed.) *Cognition: theory, research, promise*. New York, Harper & Rowe.

Youell, A. (2003) *Students entering higher education institutions with access qualifications 2002/3*. Higher Education Statistics Agency.

Younger, M., Warrington, M., Gray, J., Rudduck, J., McLellan, R., Bearne, E., Kershner, R. and Bricheno, P. (2005) *Raising boys' achievement.* London, Department for Education and Skills.

Zechmeister, J.S. and Zechmeister, E.B. (2000) Introductory psychology textbooks and psychology's core concepts. *Teaching of Psychology* **27**, 6–11.

Zinkiewicz, L., Hammond, N. and Trapp, A. (2003) *Applying psychology disciplinary knowledge to psychology teaching and learning.* York, Learning and Teaching Support Network.

INDEX